Reading & Topic-Discussion Textbook for Intermediate and Advanced Students

Let's Talk 1

Major New Edition

Written by LIS KOREA Editorial Staff
& Duane Vorhees

LIS KOREA

Introduction

Exploring Darkest English Without Map or Compass

Over the years, as LIS Korea has continued to produce its ever-expanding line of intelligent conversation guides, many people have asked for answer manuals containing the "right" answers.

With this new edition of **Let't Talk (1) (2)**, the publisher wishes to point out that the purpose of this series is not to restrict the free use of the English language, but to encourage it. English is both richly flexible and difficult for non-native users to learn because of its variability.

Most things can be correctly said in a multitude of ways that reflect the user's personality and situation; at the same time, however, the redundancy of the language generally avoids serious misinterpretation of the user's meaning, even if grievous grammatical mistakes are committed.

People who grow up with the English language are intuitive about its vagaries and, quite frankly, never bother to learn how grammarians want them to use it. Yet they may be extraordinarily expressive and eloquent in their application of it, no matter how far from "proper" they may be.

We want the users of this book to feel confident enough about their genuine ability to communicate in English, no matter how difficult the subject matter or how abstract the thought, that they will simply no longer worry about correct grammar or appropriate usage. Each section is carefully planned to allow great freedom of personal expression while also providing some definitions and explanations to help explain some of the mystery.

For the most part, the grammar is formally correct, but numerous idioms and examples of slang are also provided to indicate the richness and diversity of modern English. Feel free to explore English, boldly and fearlessly. If you get lost somewhere on the journey, don't panic—it's impossible to stay lost for very long. Just keep going ahead, and before you know it you will discover another well-lit, heavily-traficked road, and you'll be safely on your way once again!

Duane Vorhees

난산이었다. 계절이 바뀌고 있고, 한해가 저물어가는 것도 느끼지 못하며, 개정판 작업에 매달린 것이 2년여 이제 그 결실을 보게 되었다. 사실 이번 개정판 작업에서 편집진 모두는 여느 때와 달리 더욱 큰 중압감을 느꼈다. 기존 **Let's Talk (1)/(2)**는 (도서출판) 리스 코리아가 출발하면서 처음 내놓은 작품이었다. 이 작품에 대한 독자들의 사랑에 힘입어 리스 코리아가 성장해 나갈 수 있었으며 계속해서 좋은 책을 만들어 나가야 한다는 사명감을 가질 수 있었다. 따라서 더욱 발전된 책으로 보답하고자 하는 편집진의 사명은 이제까지의 어떤 책보다도 훨씬 더 진지했다. 이제 그 결실을 여러 영어학도들에게 내 놓게 됨을 매우 기쁘게 생각하며 여러분들의 격려와 비판의 목소리에 귀 기울이고자 합니다.

새롭게 개정된 Let's Talk (1) (2)의 특징은 다음과 같습니다

첫째, 현대인들의 매일매일 생활 속에 들어있는 50 개의 큰 주제 속에 수백개의 작은 질문들을 수록하여 생활 속의 어떠한 주제에 대해서도 대처 할 수 있도록 구성했습니다.

둘째, 특히 What Does It Mean?은 영어학도 여러분들의 기초적인 영어 훈련을 위하여 아주 중요한 섹션이므로 꼭 연습하시기 바랍니다. 영어를 향상시키는데 영어를 영어로 설명하는 훈련보다 더 좋은 방법은 없습니다.

셋째, 이번에 새로운 개정판에서는 기존 책들과 달리 각각의 Opinion Sample에도 질문을 달아 각각의 의견에 대해 또 한번 생각해 보는 기회를 마련 했습니다.

넷째, Part (2)에서는 Part (1) 에서 배운 내용을 다시 실제적인 토론 형식을 빌어 대화체로 구성하여 실제 토론 훈련에 도움이 되도록 했습니다.

다섯째, 책 아래부분에 보여드리는 주석은 책의 좀 어려운 부분을 상세히 쉬운 영어로 설명한 것입니다. 설사 알고 있다고 하더라도 읽어 보시면 많은 도움이 될 것을 확신합니다.

아무쪼록 이책을 통해 독자 여러분의 영어가 한단계 높아지는 계기가 마련되었으면 하는 바람입니다. 또한 이번 기회에 리스 코리아의 책을 사랑해 주시는 독자들에게 말씀 드리고 싶은 것이 있습니다. 많은 독자들께서 Answer Key에 관하여 질문을 많이 하시는데 이책에 포함된 어떠한 질문에도 여러 개의 답이 나올 수 있으며 설사 그 답이 조금 이상하더라도 그것이 큰 문제가 될 것은 없습니다. 이책의 목적은 여러분의 의견을 형성하고 표출하는데 그 목적을 둔 책으로서 책 속의 질문에 근거해서 어떤 말이든지 내 뱉을 수 있다면 이책의 목적은 이미 달성 되었다고 볼 수 있습니다.

이책이 나오기까지 애써주신 모든 분들에게 감사를 드립니다. 집필에 애써주신 리스 코리아 편집진들과 책임 집필자인 Mr. Duane Vorhees 그리고 완벽한 교정을 위해 애써주신 조은예씨에게도 감사의 말씀을 드립니다. 또한 아름다운 그림을 그려주신 박희정씨 그리고 좋은 책이 될 수 있도록 도와주신 예림칼라 디자인 팀 모두에게 감사의 말씀을 드립니다.

리스 코리아 발행인 **조 은 예**

Major New Edition

Reading & Topic-Discussion Textbook for Intermediate and Advanced Students

Let's Talk 1

CONTENTS

PART 1

25 Everyday Issues

Issue I

Single Mother's Regimen

06:00 a.m. BZZZZZ. Alarm. Brush teeth. Take a shower. Turn on TV news channel.
06:10 a.m. Make coffee and cereal.
06:15 a.m. Eat cereal and drink coffee. If I'm lucky the children don't wake up and I have 15 minutes to read the paper.
06:30 a.m. Toss clothes in washer and get children up.
06:40 a.m. Still trying to get children up.
06:45 a.m. Drag children out of bed.
06:50 a.m. Fix breakfast for kids and prepare their school lunches.
07:10 a.m. Get dressed for work.
07:20 a.m. Make sure children are dressed for school, teeth brushed, shoes tied, hair combed/brushed.
07:25 a.m. Put makeup on so I look presentable.
07:30 a.m. Makeup half on, shuffle kids out the door for school.
07:40 a.m. Drive to work.
08:15 a.m. Arrive at office. Lots of responsibility, salary only fair, but the work is interesting.
Noon. Most lunch hours I go to the dentist or shop for the kids' necessities and phone my mother.
01:00 p.m. Back to work until 5 p.m. or later.
05:00 p.m. Go to day-care center and pick up children.
05:45 p.m. Finally make it home. The traffic is terrible.
05:46 p.m. Get mail and go through past-due bills.
05:50 p.m. Start dinner, something affordable and quick. Fight children off from cookie jar.
06:00 p.m. Do breakfast dishes and set table.

- **regimen :** regular course of action
- **fix :** make (sth) ready; prepare
- **presentable :** suitable for being shown
- **shuffle :** move (sth) quickly, skillfully
- **fair :** somewhat good; acceptable
- **go through :** sort
- **past-due :** overdue; behind in payment
- **affordable :** (sth) within one's financial means

06:30 p.m. Eat dinner.
07:00 p.m. Make children do homework and take baths.
07:15 p.m. Insist that children do homework and take baths. Clean table and do dishes.
08:00 p.m. Help children finish homework.
08:30 p.m. Sit down to watch TV. Referee fights between the kids. Answer questions about sex. Explain why dad doesn't see them, why they can't have new clothes, and why they don't go skiing "like other kids."
09:00 p.m. Make children brush teeth and go to bed.
09:15 p.m. Do washing, ironing, mending, pay what I can on the bills, write stalling letters to keep creditors off my back.
10:00 p.m. Go to bed.
06:00 a.m. BZZZZZ. Alarm. Another day.

What Does It Mean?

1. look presentable
2. day-care center
3. Traffic is terrible.
4. past-due bills
5. start dinner, something affordable and quick
6. write stalling letters to keep creditors off my back

Comprehension

1. What does the woman usually do at lunch?
2. Does she do the breakfast dishes in the morning?
3. Why isn't her family financially well off?

- referee : judge or arbitrate, enforce rules or standards, decide between competing positions
- stalling letters : correspondence seeking to delay action
- get or keep off (one's) back : stop annoying or bothering (sb)

Let's Talk!

1. Why are modern people busy?
2. Do you think they are really busy or do they just pretend to be?
3. How could they have more free time?
4. Could technical developments in the future allow people to have more free time?
5. Are modern people happier than those of 30 years ago?
6. Describe your daily routine. BE AS PRECISE AS POSSIBLE.
7. What is your definition of happiness?

Opinion Samples

1. "Be careful what you wish for—you just might get it!" A generation ago, women wanted more freedom and opportunity. They wanted to have choices other than the traditional wife/mother roles. Largely, they succeeded in gaining this, in increments.

At first, women worked part-time, at low wages, to supplement the family income. They generally worked while their children were in school and managed to sustain the usual care and maintenance of the home. But, rather quickly, they began taking on more and more responsibility and earning more income. However, as responsibilities grew, less time was available for home-making; and as income grew, so did spending.

Families in which the woman stayed home fell further and further behind in the economic competition against their

- **in increments :** gradually
- **supplement :** add to
- **take on :** undertake or begin to handle (sth)

two-income peers, forcing husbands to work even harder and adding additional stress to the marriage. Families in which the wives took full-time jobs set the pace and expanded their consumption of the many new goods and services available to them, but then could not afford to allow either spouse to stop working, since they would then lose all their gains in status. The more money they made, the larger their financial responsibilities became, and the harder they had to work; and the greater became the stress. And most women were still forced to maintain the home as well as their careers.

(Q) How can we break the "vicious circle" that forces us to work and spend more, while our lives become ever more disappointing or hollow?

2. People found themselves working harder, relaxing less, and spending less time at home. Quick-fix solutions—fast food, artificial stimulants or sedatives, time-saving devices like computers and the internet, which merely provided more work opportunities—found ever greater demand. As people became more affluent, they found better homes and apartments ever further from work, and had to buy more, shinier, newer cars to take them back and forth, despite the lengthening lines of traffic.

The accumulating stress helped pull families apart. People waited longer to get married, had fewer children, spent ever less time together, and got divorced more often. The marital problems brought on even more financial burdens, and single parents found themselves balancing their professional and parental duties on a daily basis. Always one step from the abyss, the only solution they could see was to

- **peer :** person with equal standing with others, as in rank, class, or age
- **set the pace :** establish a quality others try to achieve
- **status :** social, legal, or professional position relative to that of others
- **stimulant :** drug that temporarily increases activity
- **sedative :** drug that tends to calm, moderate, or tranquilize nervousness or excitement
- **affluent :** relatively wealthy
- **ever further :** more and more distant
- **accumulate :** collect or gather (sth) together; increase
- **abyss :** the lowest or most hopeless depths; hell

earn more money in order to buy more comfort, some day. Often, their children were given more material goods, in lieu of personal contact with their parents, and their demand for the newest, most fashionable goods became insatiable. The desire for more social and economic equality between the genders resulted in more trouble and stress for everyone.

(Q) Are modern people unhappy in spite of unprecedented material wealth? Why do you think so (or not)?

3. Happiness is always a relative term. Some people seem indestructible in their joy, despite the hardships they undergo. Others never seem to achieve pleasure, no matter how pleasant their circumstances. This is an eternal paradox in the human condition.

But, socially, a deterioration of happiness seems to have beset modern mankind. Many of the simple joys of life have lost their value for most people. More and more, drugs, drink, sex, tobacco, and frenetic activity have come to define "the good life," not only among the youth but among those both younger and older as well. Sub-teens are aping the mannerisms of their older siblings—and their parents are copying the habits and styles of their children. Even the concept of being "middle-aged" is being advanced to the retirement age or beyond, and people who used to look forward to the quiet times of their "golden years" are working harder all day, partying late into the night, and deciding that they will need to work well into their retirement if they wish to avoid penury.

- **in lieu of :** instead of
- **insatiable :** impossible to satisfy; never satisfied
- **indestructible :** impossible to destroy
- **eternal :** endless or seemingly endless
- **paradox :** (sth) that seems to contain two parts that are opposite or that cannot both be true, but that are true nevertheless
- **deteriorate :** become worse or inferior in character
- **beset :** trouble persistently; harass
- **frenetic :** widely active or excited
- **ape :** imitate the actions of; mimic
- **mannerism :** habitual or characteristic way of doing (sth)
- **sibling :** brother or sister
- **penury :** poverty

One of the traditional ingredients of happiness has been an ability to reflect upon one's blessings, dream about future successes, and bask in the memory of accomplishments past. But "free time" has disappeared from the modern calendar. The coffee break has been replaced by the treadmill as a symbol of the age.

(Q) Talk about the traditional ingredients of happiness and contemporary ones. How do they differ?

- **ingredient :** element in a mixture
- **bask :** take pleasure; live happily
- **accomplishments past :** former successes
- **treadmill :** stationary device with a moving belt on which (sb) walks or runs for exercise

Issue 2

Biggest Lies

1. It's a good thing you came in today. We only have two in stock.
2. This is a very safe building. No way will you ever be burglarized
3. I promise to pay you back out of my next paycheck.
4. Five more pounds is nothing to a person with your height.
5. But officer, I only had two beers.
6. You made it yourself? I never would have guessed.
7. It's delicious, but I can't eat another bite.
8. Your hair looks just fine.
9. It's nothing to worry about—just a cold sore.
10. Now, can I go out to play? I've finished my homework.
11. The river never gets high enough to flood this property.
12. I already sent it. The delivery is on the truck.
13. Go ahead and tell me. I promise I won't get mad.
14. The ever-present line on a post card: Having a great time. Wish you were here.
15. This car is like brand-new. It was owned by two retired schoolteachers who never went anywhere.
16. The doctor will call you right back.
17. So glad you dropped by. I wasn't doing a thing.
18. You don't look a day over 40.
19. It's a very small spot. Nobody will notice.
20. The baby is just beautiful!
21. The new ownership won't affect you. The company will remain the same.

→ in stock : available; on hand
→ cold sore : open wound at the corner of the mouth

22. The puppy won't be any trouble, Mom. I promise I'll take care of it myself.
23. I'm a social drinker and I can quit any time I want to.
24. Put the map away. I know exactly how to get there.
25. You don't need it in writing. You have my personal guarantee.
26. Sorry, the work isn't ready. The computer broke down.
27. I'll do it in a minute.
28. The reason I'm so late is I ran out of gas.
29. Our children never caused us a minute's trouble.
30. The three biggest lies: I did it. I didn't do it. I can't remember.

What Does It Mean?

QUES...

1. The new ownership won't affect you.
2. social drinker
3. You don't need it in writing.
4. ever-present line

Comprehension

QUES...

1. Who tells lie No. 1?
2. Who tells lie No. 2?
3. Who tells lie No. 3?
4. Who tells lie No. 5?
5. Who tells lie No. 7?
6. Who tells lie No. 10?
7. Who tells lie No. 11?
8. Who tells lie No. 12?
9. Who tells lie No. 14?
10. Who tells lie No. 15?
11. Who tells lie No. 16?
12. Who tells lie No. 21?
13. Who tells lie No. 23?
14. Who tells lie No. 25?
15. Who tells lie No. 28?

Let's Talk!

1. Why do people lie?
2. List some white lies* you tell sometimes.
3. What was the biggest lie in your life?
4. Who lies the most often?
5. Who never tells a lie?
6. A lie begets another lie. Why?
7. How often do you lie to others?
8. How often do you lie to yourself?
9. What would happen if people started telling the truth every time?
10. How can you tell others are lying to you?

More Talking Points

What kinds of lies do they usually tell?

(a) Employees
(b) Employers
(c) Politicians
(d) Moms
(e) Dads
(f) Children
(g) Teachers
(h) Businessmen
(i) Panhandlers
(j) Newspapers
(k) Advertisements

* white lie : small, harmless fib about a small matter, often told to keep (sb's) feelings from being hurt

Opinion Samples

1. Each person has different reasons to lie. Some people do it just for fun—or they tell so-called white lies with no serious damage, and perhaps to avoid hurting someone's feelings. But problems occur when people lie to take advantage of other people's innocence in order to get material gain. This is called committing a fraud or a scam.

(Q) Do you think white lies are really harmless?

2. Politicians are the biggest liars. They promise everything they can before an election. But once they take office they do nothing to keep their promises. Why? People —the electorate—never seem to be interested in making politicians keep their promises. People seem to think that since politicians lie anyway, so they don't need to be accountable for their remarks.

(Q) Are all politicians liars? Do they need to be?

3. "We found this dog, and whoever tells the biggest lie gets to keep him."

"Well, I'm surprised at you boys! Don't you know it's wrong to tell lies? Why, I've never told a lie in my life."

"Here's the dog—you win".

(Q) What are the biggest lies people around you tell?

- **fraud :** dishonesty practiced in order to make unfair or unlawful gains
- **scam :** dishonest business scheme; swindle
- **take office :** assume an important position in government
- **electorate :** everyone qualified to vote
- **accountable :** expected or required to take responsibility for (one's) actions

Issue 3

New Year's Vows

- Let this coming year be better than any other.
- Promise to do some of the things you've always wanted to do but couldn't find the time for.
- Call a neglected friend.
- Drop an old grudge, and replace it with more pleasant memories.
- Share a funny story with someone whose spirits are dragging. A good laugh can be good medicine.
- Vow not to make any promise you don't think you can keep.
- Pay off a debt — especially one that is not monetary.
- Free yourself of some of your envy and malice.
- Encourage a young person to do his or her best.
- Share your experience and offer support. Young people need good role models.
- Make a genuine effort to stay in close touch with family and good friends.
- Resolve to stop magnifying small problems and talking without thinking.
- Find the time to be kind and thoughtful. All of us have the same allotment, 24 hours a day.
- Pay someone a compliment. It might give a badly needed lift to a person who really needs it.
- Think things through.
- Forgive a grave injustice.
- Listen more.
- Be kind.
- Apologize when you discover you were wrong. An apology never diminishes a person. It elevates him.
- Don't blow your own horn. If you've done something praiseworthy, someone will notice eventually.
- Try to understand a point of view different from your own. Nothing is 100 percent pure.

- grudge : deep-seated feeling of anger about (sth)
- drag : feel listless and exhausted; move in such a manner
- magnify : exaggerate; overstate
- think through : plan (sth) well before acting
- blow (one's) own horn : boast about (oneself)

– Examine the demands you make on others.
– Lighten up. When you feel like blowing your top, ask yourself, "Will it matter a week from today?"
– When the joke is on you, laugh the loudest.
– The surest way to have a friend is to be one. We are all connected by our humanity, and we need each other.
– Avoid malcontents and pessimists. They will drag you down and contribute nothing of value.
– Don't discourage a beginner from trying something risky. Nothing ventured means nothing gained. Losing is not as bad as not trying.
– Be optimistic. The can-do spirit is the fuel that makes things go.
– Declare war against gossip, which only causes trouble.
– Give credit when it's due. People long to be appreciated.
– Read something uplifting. Then read it to a friend.
– Don't abandon your principles, no matter how old-fashioned they appear; they never go out of style.
– Whenever courage is needed, ask yourself, "If not me, then who? If not now, when?"
– Take better care of yourself. Remember, you're all that you've got.
– Clean out your closet. Throw away the trash, give away the good stuff you don't need.
– Take those photos out of the drawer and put them in an album. Show your friends.
– If you see litter on the sidewalk, pick it up instead of walking over it.
– Give yourself a reality check. Phoniness is always transparent. It is also tiresome.
– Take pleasure in the wonders of nature. Every flower is a miracle.

- lighten up : become less serious or earnest
- blow (one's) top : become very angry
- malcontent : person who is not satisfied with current conditions
- drag (sb) down : make (sb) feel unhappy
- credit : approval or praise for some act or quality
- due : fitting or appropriate; suitable
- uplift : elevate or improve
- you've got : you have or possess
- litter : carelessly scattered scraps of paper or other waste material
- reality check : differentiation between what is genuine and what is fanciful
- phony : not genuine; fake
- transparent : easily seen through or detected

What Does It Meaning?

1. Don't blow your own horn.
2. feel like blowing your top
3. Nothing ventured means nothing gained.
4. old-fashioned principles
5. reality check

Comprehension

1. Why don't we have to blow our own horns?
2. Why should we encourage beginners to take a risk?
3. Make a list of old-fashioned principles you think are still important.

Let's Talk!

1. Why do you think people make New Year's resolutions?
2. Many people make resolutions every year. But not many succeed in keeping them. Why not?
3. What are the most popular kinds of resolutions people make?
4. What is the most difficult resolution for ordinary people to keep? Why?
5. Did you make any resolutions this year? What were they? Have you managed to keep any of them?
6. Do you always apologize if you are wrong?
7. When you hear gossip, do you spread it around or keep silent about it?
8. Why have many people abandoned old-fashioned principles?

Opinion Samples

1. Look up the word resolution. It actually means simplifying some complex problem. So, every year a lot of people resolve to do something—or to stop doing something—without much thought or analysis of the issues at stake. "I'm going to give up smoking," one person may

- resolve : make a firm decision
- at stake : at risk; in jeopardy

resolve. But nicotine is a highly addictive substance, and it is not easy to deprive oneself of that drug. It is also hard to abandon the social settings in which one usually smokes. So, the act of quitting is difficult. However, a series of relatively simple steps can be taken, each of which will make stopping easier: "I'm going to reduce my tobacco intake by one cigarette a day," for instance. "I'm going to be a better person." How? What's wrong with you now? Why are you that way, and what do you think you can do about it? "I'm going to get married." Do you have a boyfriend or girlfriend now? Why haven't you two gotten married before? What is different—or what needs to be different—this year that will make marriage more likely? Is being married the actual goal, or is it being married to an appropriate person? If you don't have a potential mate right now, how can you be sure of finding one this year? These are all practical, goal-oriented questions that need to be addressed in order to accomplish the various resolutions. Resolve by itself won't do it.

(Q) What are the urgent things for you to do to be a better person?

2. That fellow! He's the most inveterate gossip I've ever met. It seems that he knows the dirt about everyone, or at least he thinks he does. I don't think I've ever had a conversation with him in which he didn't malign at least one of our mutual friends. I don't know if he really has good information or not, but that doesn't stop him from telling it to everyone he meets. Yesterday, he told me all about Susie and her problems with her boyfriend. Did you know that she's had to get an abortion twice? If her parents knew, they would die! And her boyfriend—he's a work of art! I've never met anyone so lazy! All he does is lie around all day and "study!" I don't know what it is he's studying, but it sure isn't making any money for him.

(Q) How can we distinguish "sound criticism" from bad-mouthing?

- **deprive :** prevent (sb) or (sth) from having (sth)
- **setting :** surrounding area; environment
- **inveterate :** deep-rooted; fixed in a habit
- **malign :** speak ill of
- **work of art :** masterpiece (often used sarcastically)

Issue 4

Friends with Stress

Finding ways to reduce stress in my life is an ongoing challenge. I've always been a high-strung, driven individual, what they call a "Type-A" personality. When I'm willing to use it, the one tool that unfailingly alleviates stress for me is to surrender, give up, let go, let God or Fate act on my behalf.

Typically, I'm on my way to an appointment. Traffic is inching along because of roadwork or an accident, and I know I'll be very late. I'm getting more and more upset, to the point of physical action. My fists are clenched, my stomach is churning, I have a pounding headache, my face is becoming more and more flushed. I'm ready to blow my stack. When I finally realize how absurd my reaction is, I take a deep breath and surrender. I tell myself, "I'm in heavy traffic. There's a string of cars in front of me and another behind me, and none of them can go anywhere either. There's nothing I can do about it." So, I just accept my powerlessness and soon

- high-strung : highly sensitive or nervous
- driven : forced, pushed, not relaxed
- churn : stir or move violently
- pound : strike heavily or repeatedly
- blow (one's) stack : explode under too much pressure

become composed again.

Or perhaps I'm swimming laps in the pool. Halfway through my workout, two new swimmers start crowding my lane, occasionally bumping into me. I lose my cool and end up gulping down water. I begin to feel exhausted. Eventually, though, I see the irony in the situation: here I am, swimming to reduce stress and to enjoy myself, but the very opposite is occurring. Then I can surrender, relax, and regain my rhythm.

What Does It Mean?

1. high-strung, driven
2. to the point of physical action
3. how absurd my reaction is

Comprehension

1. What is the narrator's best tool to relieve stress?
2. How does he calm himself in heavy traffic?
3. Why is his attitude in the swimming pool ironic?

- **composed :** being in control of (one's) emotions; calm; serene
- **workout :** physical exercise
- **lose (one's) cool :** become angry or excited in a difficult situation
- **gulp :** swallow (food or liquid) greedily or rapidly in large amounts

Let's Talk!

1. What does "being friends with stress" mean?
2. What causes stress, in your case?
3. How do you cope with stress?
4. What do other people do to alleviate stress, that you know of?
5. Some people say they "enjoy" stress. What do you think they mean?
6. What kinds of stress do you cause for yourself? Which ones do others put on you?

Opinion Samples

1. Other people trying to impose their own pace on me is what causes me the most stress. I know how to get things done, but I know what my limitations are. If left alone, I know that there is nothing I can't accomplish within my field of expertise. But every task has its own personality and is not amenable to somebody's arbitrary time constraints. So when someone puts pressure on me to hurry up, I start to lose my concentration on the details, and I start to make silly mistakes, and then I have to go back and redo what I should have done right the first time. I guess I just march to the beat of a different drum and wish others would recognize that fact and let me do my own thing in my own way. We'd all be a lot happier and better off that way.

(Q) What are the advantages and disadvantages of going at one's own pace?

2. Most people are just slackers and bellyachers. They are basically lazy and don't like to be told what to do. On their own, they would never accomplish anything. Me, too, I guess, if left to my own devices. I admit it. But I respond well to pressure. The harder the job is, the better I do it. When the adrenaline starts a-flowing, I become like Superman, with no task too difficult, no job too demanding. It's like what the Marines say, "We do the difficult all the time, but the impossible just takes a little longer." So, as for me, I welcome stress, it motivates me to excel, I thrive on it, and as a result I enjoy the fruits of my success.

(Q) How is stress related to success?

- amenable : agreeable
- arbitrary : decided or arranged without any clear reason or plan, often unfairly
- constraint : limitation
- redo : do (sth) again
- do (one's) own thing : be oneself; act in a uniquely individual way; not be regimented
- slacker : person who tries to avoid work or responsibility
- bellyache : grumble or complain, especially in a whining way
- a-flowing : rushing
- demanding : requiring much effort or attention

Issue 5

Money Doesn't Guarantee Happiness

A few years ago, I shocked my friends and family. I broke my engagement to a well-educated millionaire business executive to marry a construction worker. Why? Because he's kind, honest and totally lovable. My high-school dropout can fix plumbing, tune up a car, build a house, and grow enough vegetables to feed an army. He can cook and clean like a pro, and comes home whistling every evening, without stopping at a bar. The stories about his day at the construction site are far more interesting than my day on Wall Street. This man won't grow soft and flabby sitting behind a desk all day, and he won't get a stress-related illness, or have an affair with his secretary. And if we have children, he won't be too busy to spend time with his family.

- **executive :** person that manages an organization, especially a corporation or government division
- **dropout :** person who quits high school or college
- **fix :** repair
- **tune :** repair and clean a car's engine
- **army :** large number of people
- **flabby :** having too much soft, loose fat instead of strong muscle
- **affair :** brief romantic relationship

What Does It Mean?

1. high-school dropout
2. feed an army
3. grow soft and flabby sitting behind a desk all day
4. have an affair with his secretary

Comprehension

1. How did the writer shock her family and friends?
2. Why were they surprised?
3. Describe her fiance's personality.
4. What is her job?
5. Does she think he will be a good father? If so, why?

Let's Talk!

1. Do you think she made the right decision? Why or why not?
2. Do you think money can buy happiness? If so, how? If not, why not?
3. Who is more likely to be happy, a blue-collar or white-collar worker? Why?
4. Who are happier, the rich or the poor? Why?
5. Prioritize the following things for a happy life: Money, social status, honor, friendship, health, family, respect, fame, attitude.
6. Some people say we can't be truly happy unless we develop an altruistic attitude. Do you agree?
7. Define a happy life. What can you do to achieve it?
8. Are you happy now? Why or why not?
9. What is the philosophical attitude we need to be happy?

Opinion Samples

1. The color of the collar makes all the difference in life. But the issue is not so simple, after all. Blue-collar workers perform mostly physical tasks. They work on assembly lines, in fast-food restaurants, and outdoors. Typically, their jobs do not require a college education, but they may need a great deal of training to perform successfully. Some blue-collar jobs pay extremely well, but that is usually because they are dangerous or dirty, or because they require some specialized knowledge. Payment is usually on the basis of piece-work or hourly wages.

On the other hand, white-collar workers perform their mainly mental tasks with paper or computers. They are in offices, as secretaries or managers, or in classrooms or hospitals. Most are college-educated and, generally, have higher incomes and more perks than their blue-collar colleagues. Typically, they receive salaries, though some very high-paid professionals such as doctors and lawyers are compensated per service performed.

Of course, many jobs actually blend the two aspects of "physical" and "mental" work, and the income levels mostly overlap (although blue-color incomes do not climb as far as the highest white-collar ones). The main difference is in attitude. Many people prefer active jobs in which they are constantly in motion, particularly if this entails work outdoors (in construction, for instance). They like to see and feel what they have done, and get a lot of satisfaction that way. Others are comfortable in a more sedate setting and enjoy being a vital part of the process of accomplishment rather than enjoying the actual product itself—which, in any case, may not have much of a physical presence, since it is often the drafting of a contract or a transfer of funds or some other abstraction.

(Q) Talk about the merits and demerits of blue-collar and white-collar jobs.

- **perk :** goods, privileges, or other advantages from a job in addition to the money paid
- **blend :** combine different parts or features of (sth)
- **overlap :** characteristics that simultaneously fit in more than one category
- **sedate :** calm and dignified; composed
- **abstraction :** idea or concept, rather than a physical object

2. Money may just buy more unhappiness. Most of us work too hard to acquire riches we don't need. We bust our butts↓ for eight or ten or more hours a day and have little or no time left for the things that make life worth living: personal relationships, mentally or physically engaged relaxation, contemplation↓ of our individual place in the grand scheme of things.↓ The arts, literature, music, playing games with other people, dancing, exercising, solving puzzles, self-improvement, planning for the future, dreaming about better conditions, gaining wisdom—these are the activities that define our humanity. If we are too poor or too busy to engage in them, we are no better than the other animals.

On the other hand, just having a lot of money does not guarantee that we will use our time to our best advantage. It is easy to fall into the money trap and believe that we can buy meaningful relationships or rent useful experiences. Many of the good things in life are free and available to all, but need to be nurtured;↓ they are not for sale ready-made, there is no "rich man's shortcut"↓ to their acquisition. We cannot buy self-knowledge, morality or culture; humanity is not a commodity.↓

In the end, the quality of our lives depends on no price tag. Many of the world's philosophers are poor in material possessions, not because they are too stupid to acquire riches but because they realize the ultimate poverty of empty wealth. Too many of the Fortune 500 have more money than anyone needs—and very little else.

(Q) What do you think about having a lot of money? Do you think it is an obstacle or an aid to a happy life?

- **bust (one's) butt :** work or perform to (one's) utmost
- **contemplate :** think about (sth) carefully
- **in the grand scheme of things :** as a part of a larger whole
- **nurture :** encourage or provide moral support; train; educate
- **shortcut :** route that is quicker or more direct than the one usually taken; a way of saving effort or time
- **commodity :** (sth) that can be bought or sold

Issue 6

Household Chores

Yesterday I spent two hours cleaning the kitchen from top to bottom. After supper I said to my husband, "Let's wash the dishes before we go to bed so we can wake up to a beautiful clean kitchen." He said, "Fine."

Well, after supper we looked at TV for a while and I went to make a phone call. Next thing I knew, he had gone to bed. I opened the bedroom door and asked, "What about the dishes?" He hollered, "Get off my back. The world won't come to an end if you leave the dishes till tomorrow."

I was really steamed but decided not to make a big thing out of it. I taped a note to the bedroom mirror saying, "Wake me when you get up and we'll do the supper dishes together before you go to work."

When I got up the next morning the note was gone and so was my husband. The kitchen was still a mess. I

- from top to bottom : thoroughly
- holler : yell or shout
- get off (one's) back : leave alone; stop bothering
- steam : become angry
- make a big thing out of (sth) : make (sth) seem more important than it really is, by getting angry, excited etc.

don't know whether to clean it up and pretend like nothing happened or drive like a mad woman to his office and dump the pots and pans on his desk.

We both work full-time and he promised when we married that if I kept my job we would divvy up the housework 50-50. Well, it hasn't worked out that way.

What Does It Mean?

1. I was really steamed but decided not to make a big thing out of it.
2. The kitchen was still a mess.
3. We would divvy up the housework 50-50.
4. It hasn't worked out that way.

Comprehension

1. What did the writer do yesterday?
2. What did her husband promise to do after supper?
3. When she made a phone call, what did her husband do?
4. When she woke him up, what did he say?
5. What did she do last night instead of having a big argument with him?
6. What did her husband promise to do before they married?

- divvy up : divide
- work out : develop or happen

Let's Talk!

1. Do you think it is fair to divide housework equally if both husband and wife have full-time jobs?
2. If your wife had no outside job, do you think you should help her with housework? If not, why not? If so, what kind of chores should you help her with?
3. Would you make your husband help you with the housework?
4. If your husband refused to help, what would you do?
5. Are you willing to be a househusband if your wife made more money than you?
6. Could you take pride in being married to a househusband?

Opinion Samples

1. Many women who work outside the home do all the housework because their hubby refuses to help. But as the number of working women increases, they naturally expect their husbands to help with the chores at home. Shopping, cooking, cleaning, doing dishes and laundry, and even child care must be equally shared. If not, busy wives who work won't be able to balance their time between job and house. Any wife who works outside the home has a perfect right to expect her husband to pitch in with mutual household chores.

(Q) What kinds of housework do you do on a regular basis?

2. Some people hold the following opinion: Even though a couple both work full time and are equally tired when they get home, it is still the woman's job to do the cooking, cleaning, laundry and child care. Why?

Because he earns twice as much money as she does. She should work at home to make up the wage differential.

- hubby : husband
- chores : the everyday work around the house
- pitch in : join forces with (sb); help or cooperate
- make up : compensate for (sth)

(Q) Do you think it's fair to have to do extra work just because one makes less money than one's partner?

3. Stay-at-home moms are mainly responsible for doing housework. But bring-home-a-paycheck wives have a right to ask their husbands to share in the household chores equally.

(Q) Some people say mothers who stay at home to take care of the house and family play the most important role in society. Why might this be so?

4. I am entirely responsible for the financial support of my family, but everything else is my wife's responsibility.

(Q) Is he selfish? Do you think he loves his wife?

5. I'm a newlywed, working full-time, and my husband and I have been trying to figure out how to divide our common chores. He's in construction, and by the end of the day he doesn't have enough energy left to do housework. We have tried many different ways to make a fair division of the housework, but nothing has seemed to work.

He agreed that it isn't fair that I have to do it all plus do my own nine-to-five job, so we agreed to hire a maid to come in every two weeks. Although this was affordable, I got to thinking about why I resented doing the housework in the first place—it wasn't so much that I hated the chores, but that I hated to do it for free. I thought that if I were being paid for the work, I would feel it was a real job and I wouldn't mind it so much. The "house account" now gives me $30 a week for three hours of work. I've been doing this for six months now and love the extra spending money.

(Q) Do you think this is a good solution? Why or why not? What future conflicts do you think this couple can expect?

- figure out : solve or work out
- nine-to-five job : normal-hours office job
- affordable : within (one's) financial means
- resent : feel angry at (sth) considered mean, unjust, or offensive
- mind : object to or dislike (sb) or (sth)

Issue 7

The Perfect Woman and How to Make Her

I wonder if people fully realize how women are being sabotaged by the advertising establishment, which tells us we are nothing unless our bodies are perfect.

We live in a society in which women are brainwashed to feel imperfect, because it's good business to keep selling products that (by definition, since no one is perfect) can never achieve their goal. Women have chosen to place so much importance on their weight and looks because they have been taught that if they look better, they will be better loved and have more fun.

I used to be bulimic. But after seeing a very good counselor, I realized that I'd chosen to give an insane amount of power to those extra 10 pounds on my

- sabotage : disable deliberately
- establishment : center of power and influence
- brainwash : persuade by intense means, such as repeated suggestions, to adopt a belief or behave in a certain way
- by definition : by (sth's) very nature
- bulimic : suffering from a disorder (bulimia), usually occurring in young women, caused by fear of being fat, in which (sb) eats a lot of food and then vomits it away
- insane : mentally ill

body. I know now that my life and my problems are the same whether I'm 10 pounds overweight or 10 pounds underweight. When will the media and other powerful elements in our society stop insisting that thinness is ideal? Why are women judged by what they weigh, but men are judged by what they do and the way they do it?

What Does It Mean?

QUES...

1. Women are being sabotaged by the advertising establishment.
2. Women have chosen to place so much importance on their weight and looks.

Comprehension

QUES...

1. Why does making women feel sensitive to their imperfections make good business sense?
2. What did the writer realize after seeing a counselor?
3. How are men and women judged differently? What should the common standard be?

Let's Talk!

1. Are you worried about your weight? How about your height? If so, what can you do?
2. Do you think slim people are more accepted in our society than fat ones? Why?
3. How much responsibility do the mass media have for causing dieting problems?
4. How can we win the diet war? Can it be won?
5. On what basis should the "proper" weight be determined? Who do you think should decide this?
6. What kinds of weight-control methods are available without side effects?

Opinion Samples

1. The only way to lose weight and keep it off is by changing one's eating habits and incorporating exercise into the daily routine—permanently. Young, healthy girls should not be dieting. Exercising regularly and eating well-balanced, nutritious meals should be sufficient. But, unfortunately, I see no realistic solution to this problem, since the obsession with being pencil-thin is inherent in our media culture.

(Q) Do you think that most people in the entertainment business are abnormally thin? Why should we have to copy them?

2. Study after study indicate that "the beautiful people" have significant advantages in our society: they are more popular, they get hired earlier and promoted more often, and obtain the most desirable mates. A large part of the "beauty equation" is thinness. This is a rather recent phenomenon: up until a century or so ago, voluptuousness was a positive value for women, and for men to be heavy was a sign of economic success. But, in the long run, any such emphasis on irrelevant factors as determinants of social leadership leads to dysfunction and failure; remember the Chinese civil service exams, in which the government's administrators were chosen on the basis of how well they had memorized classic Chinese poems. I fear we are heading for the same fate as the Chinese Empire, which fell into stagnation and decline, because our leaders will be picked on the basis of their looks, not their ability.

(Q) Do you think it's fair that thin people are more favored over the relatively fat ones? Why or why not?

- **keep off :** prevent from regaining
- **incorporate :** include (sth) as a part in a whole
- **inherent :** being part of the basic nature of a person or thing
- **equation :** formula
- **voluptuous :** having large breasts and a soft curved body
- **irrelevant :** having no relation to the matter at hand
- **determinant :** (sth) that strongly influences behavior
- **dysfunction :** impaired or abnormal functioning
- **head for :** move toward (sth)
- **stagnation :** condition of water not flowing, usually being foul or polluted as a result

Issue 8

Know Yourself

It can be interesting as well as useful to think about the way we define ourselves as individuals. We tend to focus on particular facets: size, gender, vocation, material possessions, family name, where we were educated or grew up, things like that.

Some of us perceive and define ourselves solely in negative terms: our incapability, unworthiness, faults, past behavior, comparing ourselves unfavorably to other people or against unrealistic ideals. If we define ourselves in such limited or deprecatory terms, we are very far indeed from true self-acceptance.

In my own case, I try to recognize and acknowledge the whole me. That includes the sum of all my experiences, good and bad. It concerns my present reality: not the me I want to be or hope to be, nor the me I think others

- facet : aspect
- gender : sexual identity
- deprecatory : expressing criticism or disapproval

see, and certainly not the former me who no longer exists. By taking a hard, cool appraisal[↓] of myself, I'm able to make sound decisions about my life and where I need to go.

What Does It Mean?

1. unrealistic ideals
2. the former me

Comprehension

1. In what ways do some people define themselves negatively?
2. What is the result of a negative definition of oneself?

→ **appraisal :** statement or opinion judging the worth, value, or condition of (sth)

Let's Talk!

1. Why is it important to know yourself? What about understanding others?
2. Define yourself. Who are you? What are you? Apply as many criteria as you can.
3. We all know it is important to know oneself. But some will argue that it is more important to know how others think of us. Do you agree? Why or why not?
4. Are the following things important when we define others?
   (a) Appearance
   (b) Gender
   (c) Profession
   (d) Money
   (e) Religion
   (f) Educational background
   (g) Lifestyle
   (h) Hobby
   (i) The place of origin or residence
5. Are they important in defining ourselves? Why or why not?

Opinion Samples

1. We should know ourselves because these are the only things we can truly know. We can't get inside anyone else's situation, we can't know what they are thinking or how deserving they are. We judge everyone and everything through the prism of our own perceptions, needs, desires, and positions. Our emotions color our reactions to the rest of the world. Autobiography is the only truth, all else is speculation.

(Q) Do you think you know yourself? Why or why not?

2. Other people are our mirrors, because we are incapable of being objective about ourselves. We are too willing to excuse our failures or exaggerate our successes to be able to see ourselves with any degree of accuracy, so we don't know how to behave. But we can see others more dispassionately, and their behavior toward us should act as a gauge of our place in society. If they always smile when they see us, we can reasonably infer that they like us. If they frown or avoid us, it's pretty clear that they don't want to be with us. Once we realize these particular facts about ourselves, we can make reasonable deductions about our actions and what we need to do to change our situation, or realize that no adjustment is necessary. If we rely merely on self-observation, we are likely to mislead ourselves based on our hopes, because we are dependent upon our own attitudes. But we can be far more honest if we watch how others treat us, since their actions are beyond our will and control; so, objectively, we can better judge ourselves through others.

(Q) Do you really think others treat us truly? What if others pretend to like us?

- **prism :** glasslike object which divides light into all colors of the spectrum
- **speculate :** assume without conclusive evidence
- **excuse :** forgive; pardon
- **dispassionate :** objective; not influenced by strong feelings or emotions
- **infer :** arrive at (an opinion or idea) based on evidence; conclude
- **frown :** facially show disapproval of (sth)
- **deduction :** reaching a conclusion by reasoning, especially from general principles

Issue 9

TV Channel

Recently my husband and I were guests in my in-laws' home, with my husband's son and daughter-in-law. My father-in-law, my husband, the son and his wife became involved in a spirited game of spades, while I watched TV in the living room. When a program came on about euthanasia, I, being of an inquisitive nature and possessing a thirst for knowledge, became quite interested.

After a few minutes came this voice from afar—it was my husband's son demanding that I change the channel! I told him I didn't want to change the channel and suggested that he concentrate on his card game. A minute or so later, he stood up and announced that he and his wife were going to bed because I refused to change the channel!

My husband was furious with me for refusing to give in — and I was angry at being ordered to change the TV channel while the card players entertained themselves as they pleased.

- euthanasia : the act of ending the life of (sb) suffering from an incurable illness or injury; mercy killing
- inquisitive : curious
- afar : a long distance away
- furious : very angry
- entertain : do (sth) that amuses or interests

What Does It Mean?

1. spirited game
2. inquisitive nature

Comprehension

1. Where did the writer go recently?
2. What did she do there?
3. What did the other family members do?
4. What was on TV that night?
5. Why was she interested in the program?
6. What did the husband's son demand?
7. What was her retort?
8. Why did the son and his wife go to bed?
9. Why was the writer's husband angry?
10. Why was the writer angry?

retort : quick, sharp reply

Let's Talk!

1. Why do you suppose the son demanded that she change the station?
2. Was it right for the son to make that demand?
3. Did her husband have good reason to be angry with her, simply because she refused to follow his son's demand?
4. Who is the most powerful person in your family in terms of TV program selection?
5. What kinds of programs do you prefer? Why?
6. Do you think TV can be educational for children? Why or why not?
7. Talk about the good programs and bad ones on TV.
8. What are the bad side effects of children watching TV?
9. Today many commercials are flooding the airwaves. Do you like them? Do you think they give you necessary information?

Opinion Samples

1. I understand the son's attitude. He thought the program on TV was not proper for a family gathering. However, I also say he had no right to order her to change the channel. It was not his home. And all the people there except the writer were enjoying themselves by playing cards, so she had a right to enjoy herself anyway she wanted.

(Q) Why couldn't she read a book instead of watching TV? Then there would be no trouble in the family.

- commercial : advertisement on radio or television
- flooding : overflowing
- gathering : meeting of group of people

2. In many families the channel-selecting power has come into the hands of the kids because of the parents' lack of responsibility. Children seem to watch everything they want. Parents tend to believe that watching TV is always educational and don't seem to consider the possible bad side effects of children being exposed to TV for long periods of time. The right to decide what to watch should be in the hands of parents. And parents should be intelligent enough to screen the children's programs and decide which is "really" educational.

(Q) Do you think it's okay to let children choose channels at their own whim?

3. When kids are watching TV they're doing nothing, since not one skill is being exercised. Television-watching inhibits initiative, curiosity, motivation, imagination, reasoning and attention span. Because the action shifts constantly in time, it also fails to promote logical, sequential thinking, thereby causing problems in following directions and anticipating consequences. And there is ample evidence that television-generation children, deprived of opportunities for discovery and developing their natural gifts, are less competent than previous generations.

I think it makes sense to keep a child away from television as much as possible until at least the third grade, when he or she has learned to read well. After that, there is no problem letting a child watch educational or sports programs, but I recommend that parents allow no more than five hours of television a week.

(Q) Why is it dangerous to let children watch too much TV?

- **side effects :** unexpected results of a situation or event
- **exposed :** not covered or protected from harm or danger
- **screen :** examine (sb) or (sth) systematically to determine suitability
- **whim :** sudden, spontaneous idea; urge
- **inhibit :** restrain or hold (sth) back; prevent
- **initiative :** the ability to make decisions and put plans into effect
- **reasoning :** logical thinking
- **span :** period of time
- **sequential :** one thing following after another
- **ample :** more than enough
- **deprive :** prevent (sb) or (sth) from having; deny

Issue 10

Dad Hates My Boyfriend

I've been seeing my boyfriend for over a year and our relationship is fantastic. We get along beautifully and have a great deal in common. This man gives me love, support, understanding, and companionship. He is the man I have been waiting for all my life. There is, however, one problem: My parents hate him. Though my mother struggles to be civil to him, my father won't allow his name to be mentioned in the house. I am beside myself trying to work this out and am having very little success. When holidays come around, my boyfriend is never included. This puts me in an awkward position because when I don't attend these functions I hurt my family. His family is wonderful to me, and they enjoy having me around. I plan to marry this terrific man, but I'm terrified about what the wedding will be like under these circumstances. My parents need to know how much they are hurting me and the person I love.

→ **beside (oneself) :** frantic; feeling strong emotion about (sth)
→ **function :** formal social gathering or official ceremony

What Does It Mean?

1. We get along beautifully and have a great deal in common.
2. My mother struggles to be civil to him.
3. I am beside myself.
4. never included

Comprehension

1. How long have they been seeing each other?
2. What is wrong with their relationship?
3. Does her mom hate the writer's boyfriend?
4. Is he usually invited to her home on holidays?
5. What about his family? Do they like her?

Let's Talk!

1. How much control should parents have in determining who their children date?

2. Analyze the following situations (take each one separately):
   - (a) He is 30 years older than the girl who loves him.
   - (b) He has been married before and has fathered several children.
   - (c) He has a prison record.
   - (d) He is a boozer.
   - (e) He has no college degree.
   - (f) He has no job.
   - (g) He is from a poor family.
   - (h) He is handicapped.
   - (i) He is of a different religion than the girl.

Opinion Samples

1. If a parent thinks his kid's friends are undesirable, he tends to try everything to prevent the relationship from continuing. But I don't think it works. It just makes the child a better liar. Once children learn that being honest only gets them into trouble, they become very good at deception. So parents should let their teens select their own friends while making it clear what the house rules are and insisting on meeting all new friends so they can get to know each other.

(Q) What advice would you give your children in choosing their friends?

boozer : alcoholic; heavy drinker

2. The relationship between young children sometimes needs to be screened by parents, and if friends are not desirable for any reason children should be kept from continuing the relationship. Young children's views of their friends are too "pure" or perhaps too stereotyped, so they have not learned how to discriminate. This could lead them to irreversible disasters in life.

(Q) Why would some kids be undesirable friends for your children?

3. If I were in love with a man who treated me great, I'd marry him even if he were an ex-convict. That would mean he has paid his debt to society. So I think my parents should have no reason to turn against him, simply because there is a possibility that he might break the law again. Prison is supposed to teach people that they will be punished for illegal actions. And I would tell my parents about his record before I married him, because I know they would learn of it later on, and then we would both lose their confidence and trust. And speaking the truth would speak well for both of us.

(Q) Would an ex-convict be okay as your spouse? What should society do to (or for) ex-convicts? Do you think they are discriminated against in our society? If so, why and how?

- screen : examine (sb) or (sth) systematically to determine suitability
- stereotype : conventional or oversimplified idea or image of (sb), often based on race, gender, religion, or profession
- discriminate : detect differences, esp. in terms of quality
- irreversible : impossible to turn around
- ex-convict : former prisoner
- turn against : be unfriendly toward
- record : past actions
- speak well : say good things
- discriminate (against) : treat unfairly, especially because of prejudice based on race, sex, religion, etc.

Issue 11

Thanksgiving Every Day

– Even though I clutch my blanket and mutter when the alarm clock rings each morning, thank you, Lord, that I can hear it. There are many who are deaf.

– Even though I keep my eyes tightly closed against the morning light as long as possible, thank you, Lord, that I can see. There are many who are blind.

– Even though I huddle in my bed because I don't want to get up, thank you, Lord, that I have the strength to rise. There are many who are bedridden.

– Even though the first hour of my day is hectic, when my daughter can't find a pair of socks, when my wife burns my toast and my son hogs the bathroom, when everybody's temper is short, thank you, Lord, for my family. There are many who are lonely.

– Even though our breakfast table never looks like the pictures in magazines and the menu is at times unbalanced, thank you, Lord, for the food we

- **mutter :** complain or grumble
- **huddle :** draw (one's) limbs close to (one's) body
- **bedridden :** having to stay in bed because of sickness or weakness
- **hectic :** full of intense activity, confusion, or excitement
- **hog :** keep or use all of (sth); occupy exclusively
- **short :** get angry very easily

have. There are many who are hungry.

- Even though my job is often monotonous, thank you, Lord, for the opportunity to work. There are many who are jobless.
- Even though I grumble and bemoan my fate from day to day and wish my circumstances were not so modest, thank you, Lord, for the gift of life.

What Does It Mean?

1. clutch my blanket and mutter
2. who are bedridden
3. temper is short
4. never looks like the pictures in magazines
5. menu is at times unbalanced

Comprehension

1. Describe the writer's attitude toward life.
2. What is worse than having a bad job?
3. Describe a typical morning in the writer's life.

- **monotonous :** never different or interesting; unchanging and dull
- **bemoan :** mourn over (sb/sth); grieve for; complain about
- **modest :** limited in amount, extent, etc.

Let's Talk!

1. Are you happy with your present circumstances? How would you improve them, if you could?
2. Do you always view things optimistically? Explain your answer.
3. What do you think constitutes a happy life?
4. What do you hate most about your life? (Your job? Your family? Your English ability? Your friends? Your home?) What is wrong in that regard, and how could it be better?
5. What do you want to accomplish in life?

Opinion Samples

1. Do you know what a "Pollyanna" is? It's someone who always finds the bright side to every problem. If he loses his job, he'd say, "Well, now I have some free time." If his girl friend would break off their relationship, he'd insist that he was lucky it happened before they got married. If he broke his leg, he'd be glad that it wasn't both legs! No matter how severe the tragedy, he'd put some positive spin on it. I think people like this are foolishly optimistic. They are unrealistic in their attitudes. There is absolutely nothing wrong with being an optimist, but like anything else it can be taken too far. The main problem with it is that a Pollyanna is too content to leave things the way they are, "because they're not so bad," rather than recognize the severity of the situation and then do something about it!

(Q) What are the good points of being a Pollyanna? And what are the good points of being pessimistic?

- **constitute :** form (sth) from parts
- **spin :** the way (sb) thinks about a particular subject or the attitude he has toward it

2. I hate my job! It's the same thing every day. I get up at the same time, I get dressed and eat breakfast, I drive to work along the same route, and then the clock starts ticking on the job exactly at 9:00 every morning. I shuffle an identical series of papers every day, and at noon I go to eat with my usual colleagues in the same cafeteria, and at 1:00 I have the same papers to process until 5:00. Then I go home and watch TV and eat supper and go to bed. The next day, it all cycles through the same way. I'm in a rut.

There are some things I could do differently, I suppose. I could vary my activities at home and maybe go out more in the evening. But these are minor, cosmetic changes. The main source of displeasure in my life is my dratted job! There just isn't much I can do to change the basic nature of the routine. And, what's worse, it's all my own fault that I'm trapped in my profession! I spent years in school, training for it. I worked hard and studied assiduously for years, and then I went to a dozen interviews before I was hired. But now, I find that I hate this occupation, and I'm stuck in it! I can't do anything else.

(Q) How many people do you think are happy with their jobs? If they are not, what alternatives do they have?

- **shuffle :** rearrange (objects, etc.) by mixing together randomly
- **in a rut :** in a fixed, usually boring, routine
- **cosmetic :** dealing with the outside appearance rather than the important part of (sth)
- **dratted :** euphemism for "damned"
- **trapped :** caught
- **assiduous :** diligent

Issue 12

Lower Your Expectations

When you expect too much from life, when you are unrealistic but overly demanding, you set yourself up for disappointment and a great deal of unnecessary grief. You'll probably also alienate at least some of those you work with, because most people don't appreciate being held to unrealistic expectations. You may want the events in your life to evolve in a certain, predictable way, and people to behave according to your plans for them. But if they don't, as is often the case, you end up feeling stressed out and miserable.

Life is just not neat and trouble-free. People make mistakes, and we all have bad days. Sometimes people are rude or insensitive. No job is entirely secure, and no matter how much money you

- overly : excessively
- demanding : requiring much effort or attention
- set up : prepare
- alienate : lose the friendship or support of (sb); cause (sb) to become emotionally isolated
- as is often the case : in the normal course of events
- end up : come to a finish or a final position

make, it probably doesn't seem enough. Phone lines and computers occasionally break down, along with everything else.

Often, just simply by lowering your expectations, however slightly, you can make your day (and your life) seem a whole lot easier. You can create an emotional environment for yourself whereby, when things work out well, you'll be pleasantly surprised and grateful. And if your plan doesn't work out exactly, it won't devastate you. Instead of reacting negatively, you'll be able to say, "Oh well, I can handle it." Keeping your composure allows you to deal with the irritant or solve the problem, whatever it is, as well as you can under the circumstances, and be done with it.

What Does It Mean?

1. Most people don't appreciate being held to unrealistic expectations.
2. as is often the case
3. be done with it

Comprehension

1. What happens if you expect too much?
2. What are the advantages of lowering your expectations?

- **devastate :** overwhelm (sb); harm
- **composure :** control over (one's) emotions; calmness
- **irritant :** (sth) that bothers
- **under the circumstances :** insofar as the situation permits

Let's Talk!

1. Why do we expect certain things from others?
2. Is it easy to lower our expectations? Why or why not?
3. What is a good approach to lowering your expectations, in your opinion?
4. What would happen if life were trouble-free?

More Talking Points

Answer each of these questions based on the list below.

1. What are your expectations in regards to _______?
2. Are your expectations always realized by ________?
3. In what ways do(es) ______ fail to satisfy your expectations?
4. How do you cope with disappointment in this case?

(a) Sweetheart
(b) Friends
(c) Parents
(d) Children
(e) Your school
(f) Your company
(g) Your boss
(h) Your co-workers
(i) Politicians
(j) Government
(k) Yourself

Opinion Samples

1. The lowering of expectations is the fastest path to mediocrity and failure. Only by setting standards higher than our current level of achievement can we raise ourselves up. Most people already have an adequate number of justifications for their lack of success—they certainly do not need one more. What the ambitious ones among us must do to fulfill ourselves is to aim for the very top and then keep advancing to that point without letup. The rest of you can settle for less if you prefer—it just makes my own march easier that way.

(Q) Who/What raises your expectations? Who/What lowers your expectations?

2. Some unfortunate souls sink at the first squall, often through no fault of their own. Others seem to glide effortlessly through life, with no dark cloud ever smudging their horizon. But their blessed existences live for nothing beyond themselves. The ones who accomplish the most, and who are remembered the longest, are the masters of adversity, who stand up fearlessly to all comers, who may be knocked repeatedly down but still keep getting back up.

(Q) Why is it important to struggle against adversity?

- **mediocre :** neither good nor bad; average
- **letup :** reduction in pace, force, or intensity
- **squall :** sudden storm, esp. at sea
- **smudge :** make a dirty mark on a surface
- **comer :** anyone who approaches

Issue 13

Positively Negative

– We drink out of joy but become miserable.
– We drink for sociability but grow argumentative.
– We drink for sophistication but become crude.
– We drink for friendship but make enemies.
– We drink to go to sleep and awaken exhausted.
– We drink for strength but feel weak.
– We drink to be exhilarated and end up depressed.
– We drink for "medicinal purposes" and acquire health problems.
– We drink to calm down but end with the shakes.
– We drink to get confidence and get more afraid.
– We drink to make conversation flow more easily, and the words come out slurred and incoherent.
– We drink to diminish our problems and see them multiply.
– We drink to feel heavenly and end up feeling like hell.
– We drink to cope with life and invite death.

What Does It Mean?

1. We drink for "medicinal purposes."
2. We drink to make conversation flow more easily.

- **sociability :** friendliness, esp. being part of a crowd
- **argumentative :** quarrelsome
- **crude :** primitive
- **slur :** pronounce carelessly or indistinctly
- **incoherent :** lacking order or logical connection
- **multiply :** increase in number or amount

Comprehension

QUES...

1. Does drinking help cultivate sociability? What do you mean by your answer?
2. How can drinking for medicinal purposes lead to health problems?

Let's Talk!

Do you agree? Why or why not?

1. We ask for advice but are not ready to take it.
2. We spank our children to educate them, and they learn that violence can solve all conflicts.
3. We try to persuade somebody, and he just becomes more stubborn.
4. We make money to live well, and the money makes us sick.
5. We work hard for a comfortable old age, and health problems lead us to "early retirement."
6. We produce children to make our lives happy, and they become our biggest troubles.
7. We read the newspapers for their objectivity and become ever more biased.
8. We buy lottery tickets to get rich and lose money every time we buy them.
9. We adopt our religion to find peace and learn to fight against other beliefs.
10. We punish lawbreakers, and they become more criminal.
11. We destroy nature to make money but have to pay three times the amount to restore the environment.
12. For the sake of our friendship, we give money to a friend and then we lose them both.
13. Every confidence proves but a prejudice.

→ **cultivate :** develop
→ **stubborn :** strong-willed, determined
→ **objective :** not influenced by (one's) own feelings or opinions in the making of a judgment or decision
→ **biased :** prejudiced
→ **prejudice :** judgment or opinion formed before the facts are known

Opinion Samples

1. Since there is only one God, and only one Word of God, it follows that all other religious ideas are wrong. Though others may have a right to be wrong, it is our duty to set them aright. We are commanded by God to bring salvation to the unbelievers, so they must be forced to accept the One Truth for their own good. It is wrong to ignore evil, or it will multiply, so we have an obligation to spread the Truth.

"Moderation" is just a sign of moral laxity, so we must exert every effort. Religious dissension will end only when the false religions disappear; only then will moral peace descend upon the Earth.

(Q) Is it possible for mankind to have only one religion? If so, would this lead to permanent world peace?

2. I get up in the morning and look myself in the face. Well, actually, of course, I look at myself in the mirror. And the mirror, by its very nature, always lies: the right is whatever is left. But I try to use the mirror to imagine what I really look like to the other inhabitants of the planet. Sometimes I have to squint a bit to get the proper perspective, and naturally I can't see my hair thinning behind, or the thickening waist below the frame. And if I can't see them, they don't exist, do they? And neither can I see within—but the insides are safe from anyone's casual inspection (thank God!). I can only hope that the image I project matches the one the world receives. After thoroughly reflecting upon myself and my proper place, I go out into society.

(Q) Can people match their appearance with their interior being?

- **it follows :** it must be true
- **set them aright :** make them correct
- **salvation :** the saving of the soul from sin and punishment
- **moderation :** the quality of not being extreme
- **lax :** not firm; loose
- **dissension :** difference of opinion; disagreement
- **descend :** move from a higher to a lower place
- **squint :** look with the eyes partly closed

3. We are constantly fooled by our senses—mirages present us with places that don't exist, spoons appear to bend in a glass of water, we hallucinate, we sometimes fail (or refuse) to see the obvious. The world is not as it seems. The famous philosopher Descartes once set out to reject everything he could not be sure of. Eventually he decided that, because thinking the problem through to its logical limits implied "a thinker," he could not doubt the existence of himself as a thinking being. "I think, therefore I am," he proclaimed. But later philosophers rejected even that minimum: How can we know that we exist, since we might just be part of someone else's dream? But this notion at least implies that some dreamer exists somewhere; we just can't be sure about our own independent being. Even this supposition has been dismissed by further skeptics, who insist that systems of belief can only be objectively proved or disproved from outside themselves; everything within the system works on the assumption that it "is," but its reality cannot be demonstrated. The tools of mathematics cannot be used to verify its own objective truth. All is supposition, nothing is real beyond doubt. Doubt itself is but a posture.

(Q) How do you know what the truth is?

- **mirage :** image (one) sees, esp. in the desert, of an object that is not present
- **hallucinate :** see things which do not exist
- **set out :** start
- **work :** operate
- **posture :** the way (one) behaves or thinks in a particular situation

Issue 14

Pet People and Their Trouble

Our son, daughter-in-law, and grandson accepted our invitation for a Memorial Day cookout. They live about a 45-minute drive from our home. Our daughter-in-law somewhat reluctantly agreed to leave their dog home, knowing that my wife and I are not "pet people."

Memorial Day morning, she telephoned to say that she was sorry, but she just couldn't leave the dog alone all day. Then she said that the dog was a member of their family. She probably expected me to cave in and say, "Well, all right. Bring the dog." Instead I said, "I'm sorry you're not coming, but I understand your feelings. Perhaps another time." She said, "Well, goodbye," and then she hung up. Neither she nor my son has communicated with us since.

What Does It Mean?

1. cookout
2. pet people

Comprehension

1. What were the family going to do?
2. How far away does the son's family live?
3. Do the grandparents like pets?
4. Does the son's family like pets?
5. Why did the daughter-in-law telephone the grandparents?
6. Why haven't the son and daughter-in-law telephoned again?

- **Memorial Day :** holiday to commemorate the dead, esp. those who died in war
- **reluctant :** unwilling
- **cave in :** yield; surrender; give in

Let's Talk!

1. Who do you think was wrong?
2. Who do you think should break the silence first?
3. What do you think about people who take their pets to restaurants and supermarkets?
4. Having pets in an apartment is illegal. What do you think about that law?
5. People who complain about barking say dogs should be operated on to be made mute. What do you think about this idea? Is it too cruel? Who has greater rights, people or dogs?
6. Do you think eating dog meat should be understood as a dietary custom like any other, or as a barbarous habit that should be rooted out?

Opinion Samples

1. Who was right or wrong is unimportant. The writer has a right to ban pets from his home, and the daughter-in-law has the right to decline his invitation unless she can bring her dog. The important issue here is maintaining friendly relationships among family members.

(Q) Do you think both parties have the same rights?

2. I understand the writer had a right to say "no." But if the parents had said "yes," they might have seemed more generous to their children and grandchildren, and there wouldn't have been any estrangement. The party was just for a few hours. If we want to have good relations with people, sometimes we have to endure some unpleasantness.

(Q) Do you ever have to endure unpleasant things in order to maintain good relationships with other people? Give us an example.

- **break the silence :** begin communicating
- **estrangement :** unfriendly or hostile situation, esp. among those who would normally be expected to be close

Issue 15

Can You Please Put Out Your Cigarette?

[A]

"Excuse me? Can you please put out your cigarette? You are disturbing me." Nowadays many cities and nations are imposing curbs that restrict smoking in most public places. As antismoking campaigns in the U.S. and Singapore have demonstrated, tough laws and peer pressure can fast reduce the smoker from being an admired sophisticate to becoming a social pariah. Throughout Europe and Asia, a growing body of laws, policies, and guidelines is confining smokers to ever-smaller zones. France has prohibited all tobacco advertising. And in the developing countries of Asia, a mounting awareness of the ill effects of smoking is prodding governments there to act as well.

Not surprisingly, Singapore is striving to become the world's first smoke-free city. In this socially engineered ministate, where even chewing gum is banned, smoking has been under assault for two decades; cigarettes are strictly banned in nearly every public place, vending machines are outlawed, and tobacco companies are not allowed to sponsor public events.

As the economies of other Asian nations thrive, their citizens pay more attention to their health and push for tougher smoking regulations. Even China, the world's largest producer and consumer of tobacco, restricts smoking in public places and bans cigarette advertising.

None of this means that smokers need to

- curb : control or limit
- peer pressure : strong feeling that (sb) must behave the same way as other people of the same group in order to be accepted or popular
- reduce : bring (sth) into a lower or worse condition or state
- sophisticate : urbane, refined person
- pariah : (one) who has been excluded from society; outcast
- mounting : increasing; growing higher
- prod : stir to action; urge
- assault : violent physical or verbal attack
- ban : prohibit by law, decree, or rule
- vending machine : push-button device that sells small objects such as cigarettes, chocolate, or coffee
- outlaw : declare (sth) illegal
- thrive : make steady progress; prosper

fear extinction anytime soon. Cigarettes are still highly profitable, as the governments of France, Italy, and Japan know, since they monopolize or control state tobacco industries. Private U.S. companies are making up for dwindling domestic sales by expanding marketing abroad. Asian health officials complain that the influx of fancy foreign brands hurts their efforts to control the habit, particularly among the young.

[B]

Quitting smoking is generally something to celebrate, but for many ex-smokers there is a heavy price to pay on the scales. A study by the U.S. Center for Disease Control confirmed what many former smokers have learned from experience: Americans who swear off smoking can expect to gain weight—an average of 3.8 kg for women, 2.8 kg for men. More disturbing is the finding that 1 in 8 women who quit—and 1 in 10 male quitters—add a hefty 13 kg or more, while continuing smokers tend to gain much less. Health officials are concerned that the desire to stay slim may contribute to the high rate of smoking among American teenage girls, who tend to take up the habit at a younger age than boys. The American Journal of Public Health has reported that more than twice as many adolescent girls as boys said they were worried about gaining weight if they quit smoking. Naturally, cigarette companies capitalize on such fears. Unfortunately, doctors note, even modest weight gains can loom large for women: a gain of 3.8 kg, for instance, can translate into a different dress size; for men it may mean only letting the belt out a notch.

- **extinct :** no longer existing
- **monopoly :** complete control over the making or selling of a product or service
- **monopolize :** dominate by oneself; gain or have a monopoly over (sth)
- **dwindle :** become smaller; diminish
- **influx :** arrival of people or things, esp. in large numbers
- **swear off :** promise to give up (sth)
- **hefty :** large, heavy
- **take up :** develop an interest in or devotion to (sth)
- **capitalize on :** turn (sth) to advantage ; profit by
- **loom :** come into view, often with a threatening appearance
- **notch :** hole or degree

What Does It Mean?

1. A mounting awareness of the ill effects of smoking is prodding governments to act.
2. Private U.S. companies are making up for dwindling domestic sales by expanding marketing abroad.
3. fancy foreign brands
4. a heavy price to pay on the scales
5. The desire to stay slim may contribute to the high rate of smoking among American teenage girls.

Comprehension

[A]

1. Which country or countries have banned all tobacco advertisements?
2. Which country or countries have outlawed cigarette vending machines?
3. What is the main reason many developing countries are putting mounting pressure on smokers?
4. Smokers don't have to worry about extinction anytime soon. Why not?
5. How are U.S. tobacco companies coping with declining domestic sales?

[B]

1. How much average weight gain may ex-smokers expect?
2. Are these weight gains as serious as smokers imagine?

Let's Talk!

1. Do you agree that all public places, such as restaurants, should be declared non-smoking areas?
2. Is it okay to impose drastic tax increases on cigarettes, which naturally leads to increased prices?
3. Do you think cigarette vending machines should be outlawed, since they give children easy access to tobacco products?
4. You know smoking can cause numerous kinds of diseases, such as lung cancer. So do you think it is fair to make smokers pay higher health insurance premiums?
5. Do you think it's OK for non-smokers to be given employment advantages?
6. Do you think a spouse should have the right to file for divorce in case he (or she) or the children are disturbed by secondhand smoke?
7. What do you think about a total ban on tobacco advertising?
8. What do you think about putting stronger warning labels on cigarette packs, such as running a before-and-after picture of a once-beautiful woman vomiting and bald from radiation therapy for her cancer?
9. If your boyfriend or girlfriend were a chain smoker, would you marry him or her?
10. Do you think parents have the right to tell their children to stop smoking?
11. What do you think is the most polite and least offensive way of asking someone to extinguish a cigarette in your presence?
12. What do you think is the best way to quit smoking?
13. What do you think about making smoking illegal?
14. If your child asked you for permission to smoke, what would you do?
15. Are there any good ways to deter youngsters from touching cigarettes?

- insurance premium : the amount paid or payable for an insurance policy
- therapy : treatment of disease, injury, or disability
- deter : prevent or discourage (sb)

Opinion Samples

1. I quit smoking 12 years ago—cold turkey. I'm tired of those crybabies who say they can't quit. There are only two things required to quit smoking—a sincere desire to quit, and never putting another cigarette in your mouth. People who say they want to quit but keep smoking are lying to themselves. They really don't want to quit. Please, notice that I use the term "quit"—not "stop." When you quit, it's over. When you merely stop, you usually start again. This may sound like semantics, but it helps to keep things in perspective.

(Q) What's the implied difference between those who quit smoking and those who don't?

2. Many youngsters seem convinced that smoking makes them look more sophisticated and helps them stay thin. But they never seem concerned about what it might do to their health. Smoking doesn't keep them thin, and their persistent coughs and the wrinkles around their mouth doesn't make them look very sophisticated. They are just potential cancer patients. Most teenagers don't give a thought to long-term effects. But it is the parents' responsibility to lay down the law, and those who don't fail their children badly.

(Q) Do you think smokers look cool and sophisticated? Do you think they have to smoke in order to maintain their appearance? Do you know any "cool" people who do not smoke?

3. Millions of people who consider themselves non-smokers should think again. If they allow smoking in their homes, they are smokers whether they like it or not.

I have never smoked, but I have been exposed to secondhand smoke since early childhood. Last fall I was diagnosed with lung cancer. I had major surgery followed

- **cold turkey :** immediate, complete withdrawal from (sth) on which one has become dependent, such as an addictive drug
- **crybaby :** person who complains too much, usually in a whining manner
- **semantics :** meaning, or interpretation of meaning, of a word, sign, sentence, etc.
- **keep (sth) in perspective :** maintaining the proper importance of (sth) relative to the entire situation
- **diagnosed :** medically identified

by five horrific months of chemotherapy. My weight dropped drastically. I lost all my hair, had hallucinations and nightmares, and wanted to die. All to no avail, as it turns out, since the treatment failed. To have gone through all this hell when I've never smoked a cigarette has made me very bitter.

I experienced no symptoms. My cancer was discovered during a routine medical examination. Then, a few weeks ago, I was told to get my life in order, because there isn't much time left. I'm the mother of two young children and I don't deserve to die this way since I never smoked—at least that's what I thought.

(Q) Do you think a smoker has a right to smoke in the presence of his family (even if it may harm them)?

4. My present predicament is that I met a wonderful man who wants to marry me, but there's a problem: He's a heavy smoker. He has asthma and bronchitis, and when he lights up he coughs, which makes me cringe. He keeps saying he's going to quit, but he's still smoking. He says that not everybody who smokes gets lung cancer. I feel as though he's killing himself, and there's nothing I can do about it. Should I continue to see him and hope he'll quit smoking? Or should I go on like this and fall more deeply in love with him, only to watch him die an agonizing death from lung cancer? So far I'm distancing myself from him until I know what to do.

(Q) If you were in love with a man or woman who smokes, would you marry that person?

5. I was a closet smoker who went through a pack a day for 20 years and tried to quit dozens of times. I failed because I felt I was depriving myself of a great deal of pleasure, even though I knew in my heart that cigarettes

- chemotherapy : cancer treatment using specific chemical agents or drugs that are selectively destructive of malignant cells and tissues
- to no avail : without success
- symptom : sign of disorder or disease, especially a change from normal bodily function, feeling, or appearance
- predicament : situation, especially an unpleasant or troubling one, from which it is difficult to remove oneself
- cringe : pull oneself back, as in fear or embarrassment
- distancing from : treating (sb/sth) coldly or in an unfriendly manner
- closet : secret, hidden, or private

were killing me.

What I was really experiencing was a healing crisis. Those withdrawal symptoms I felt were just the way my body purged itself of the toxins that had built up over two decades of addiction.

Each crisis lasted only about 30 seconds—just long enough to pull out a cigarette, light it and take a couple of drags. I decided to change my attitude and do something good for myself in those 30 seconds. I did 20 push-ups and occupied my hands and my mind during the crisis periods. The result? I developed a great set of pecs and haven't touched a cigarette in over four years.

When it comes to self-control I am at the bottom of the heap. So if this method worked for me, it can work for you.

(Q) Do you know any effective way to quit smoking?

6. I know there are people crying out to make smoking illegal. If that's the case, why don't we just declare all the things that some people consider undesirable to be against the law? The first thing that comes to mind is alcohol. It certainly harms far more people than smoking and in more serious ways. If we look at the damage done by drunk drivers alone, smoking, by comparison, doesn't make a dent.

Let's ban sex, too, while we're at it. Lord knows, sex can be hazardous to a person's health, what with all the diseases it can spread and the billions of dollars it costs our nation. Sex can be dangerous even if one doesn't get a disease. Consider the fact that sex can result in children, who sometimes turn out to be very expensive as well as harmful to their parents' mental health. Just the anxiety of taking care of children is enough to cause parents to smoke and drink.

Where do you draw the line? Can't we be allowed to

- **withdrawal symptoms :** physical and behavioral symptoms following cessation of continuous use of an addictive drug
- **purge :** cleanse; purify
- **drag :** puff or inhalation of a cigarette, pipe, etc.
- **pecs :** pectorals; the main chest muscles
- **bottom of the heap :** lowest in a pile
- **dent :** small damage
- **while we're at it :** while we are in the process of doing (sth)
- **hazardous :** full of danger; risky
- **draw the line :** mark an exclusion

enjoy potentially risky activities if we choose to do so of our own free will? Do we really want to live in a Big Brother dictatorship that overprotects us?

(Q) What would happen if we made smoking illegal?

7. I have an answer for the smokers who keep whining because they're treated like second-class citizens. Now you know how it feels!

I'm 50 years old and for 30 years I was considered a whiner because I didn't like smoke in restaurants, other people's homes, the teachers' lounge at school, and blowing in my face at the ballpark. The attitude was, "If you don't like it—move!"

Now that smoking is being banned from public buildings, vehicles and restaurants, it is the smokers who are complaining.

Smokers who are trying to quit have my sympathy. I know smoking is one of the hardest addictions to kick. But they can shiver outside the office building, get wet in the rain while huddling under the overhang, and fidget on the airplane, and I don't feel at all sorry for them. In 30 years we'll talk and, if they're still alive, maybe we'll compromise then. It's my turn, guys!

(Q) What do you think about banning smoking in all public places?

8. If my daughter never gave me a Christmas, birthday or Mother's Day present ever again, it wouldn't matter. She and her brother, Bill, gave me the greatest gift of all. When they were nine and 10, they began seeing TV ads about the dangers of smoking. They started taking our cigarette packs, their dad's and mine, and hiding them in a cookie jar or some other unlikely place. They made drawings of skulls and crossbones with captions such as, "Please, Mom, STOP SMOKING, please."

- **whine :** complain or protest in a childish, noisy way
- **huddle :** crowd together, as from cold or fear
- **overhang :** upper part of a building, roof, or balcony
- **fidget :** behave nervously
- **compromise :** settle a difference by having all parties agree on less than what they want

We thought it was cute at first but soon discovered they were dead↓ serious. Finally, we made an agreement. If we stopped, they would never start. It is still a true and lasting↓ gift of love 26 years later.

(Q) If your children asked you to quit smoking, would you accept their plea?

9. If the government wanted a really effective health warning about tobacco products, it would place the following message on cigarette packs: "Warning: Smoking can reduce the enjoyment and frequency of sexual activity."

(Q) Do you think it would bring the expected result? Why or why not?

10. If my child asks me for permission to smoke, I'll ask him or her to research the effects of smoking and then write me an essay accompanied by photographs. This will be a fine example of parents teaching kids how to decide things on their own, instead of merely forbidding something they believe to be destructive. It has four steps. First, identify the problem. Second, look at the alternatives. Third, weigh the consequences. Fourth, reach a decision..

(Q) What do you think is better, preventing children from harming themselves or giving them a choice?

11. I had a dream that was so vivid and so frightening that when I woke up, tears were streaming down my face. I knew I must stop my self-destructive habit once and for all.↓ I dreamed I was in a hospital dying of lung cancer and my little boy (who was two at the time) was standing by the bed crying, "Don't leave me, Daddy!"

That was enough for me. It wasn't easy, because nicotine is as powerful an addictive as heroin. But I did it, cold turkey, and since that day, I have never smoked another cigarette.

- dead : completely; absolutely
- last : continue over time; go on; persevere
- once and for all : decisively; finally

If you can't quit for yourself, quit for those who love you.

(Q) Do you think smokers are scared of developing lung cancer or other diseases? Should they be?

Issue 16

Working Mom vs Non-Working Mom

[A]

I have a 2-year-old and a baby of 6 months. I decided to go back to work and pay my aunt to take care of the children. I made this decision for two reasons: because I thought it in the best interests of the children and because I believed it would be better for me.

For one thing, my job makes it possible for my children to have excellent health insurance. Anyone who doesn't have health insurance is in real danger.

Second, I want my children to have the same quality education that I had. Do you have any idea what first-class schools cost today? Well, they are over $20,000 a year, not including room and board. I'm talking NOW. What do you think they will cost in 16 years?

I don't want anyone looking at me funny because I choose not to stay home with my children. I'm a realist, and this is the real world.

[B]

A working mom should sit in a quiet corner for an hour or two and get her priorities straight. Her children grow a little every day, and before she knows it, they will be gone. When that happens she can walk away from home and work all she wants.

Eating red beans and rice will seem like filet Mignon if she cooks for a family that loves her. The mended clothes will seem like robes of velvet and gold to her children because their mother made them. The old car will shine like a limousine if Mom is taking the kids to the library or to the park.

I believe the reason so many children are in bad shape

→ **quality :** excellent; superior
→ **realist :** (one) with interest in or concern for things that are actual rather than imaginary
→ **filet Mignon :** small tender round piece of steak cut from the thick end of a beef tenderloin

today is because they haven't had adequate parental care, they haven't felt valued and loved. What in the world could be as important as being at home for your kids? When I hear women say they want a higher standard of living for their children I ask myself, what does that really mean? A better neighborhood? Private schools? Better clothes? How important are those things?

[C]

Some women have to work. They need extra money or they're supporting their family on their own. Some women want to work. They love their families, but the daily domestic scene is not enough for them emotionally or psychologically. They prefer the challenge of the business or professional world. Good for them!

Some women prefer to stay home. They enjoy housekeeping, cooking, and being a full-time mother. This is very hard work, but they find it fulfilling. Good for them!

Not all women who work outside the home are pampered executives with painted fingernails, designer clothes, neglected husbands, and latchkey kids. Neither are all housewives brainless, frumpy women who walk around in their housecoats and curlers, saying, "Yes, dear," to their husbands and yelling at their kids.

We are all free to choose what we want to be. Be grateful. Most of our mothers and grandmothers didn't have a choice.

Hooray for the stay-at-home woman! Hooray for the career woman! Do as you please, but don't belittle the woman who chooses the other road.

- **pamper :** treat with too much kindness or care
- **latchkey kid :** child who spends part of the day alone and unsupervised, esp. one with a key to enter home after school while the parents are at work
- **brainless :** unintelligent; stupid
- **frumpy :** unattractive in dress or appearance
- **curler :** small device used to curl hair
- **belittle :** speak of (sb) or (sth) as small or unimportant

What Does It Mean?

1. not including room and board
2. get priorities straight
3. Eating red beans and rice will seem like filet Mignon if she cooks for a family that loves her.
4. So many children are in bad shape today.
5. The daily domestic scene is not enough.
6. pampered executives with painted fingernails, designer clothes, neglected husbands, and latchkey kids
7. brainless, frumpy women who walk around in their housecoats and curlers saying, "Yes, dear," to their husbands and yelling at their kids
8. Most of our mothers and grandmothers didn't have a choice.
9. Don't belittle the woman who chooses the other road.

Comprehension

[A]
1. What made the woman decide to go back to work?
2. What does her job allow her children to have?
3. What does the writer think the top priority is, for her children?

[B]
1. When does the writer think is the right time for moms to go to work?
2. Why are children today in such bad shape?
3. Does the writer think a higher living standard is important?

[C]
1. Why do some women work?
2. Why do some women prefer to stay at home?
3. What do many people think about career women?
4. What do many people think about stay-at-home women?

Let's Talk!

1. Would you prefer being a career woman or a housewife? Why?
2. Do you want your wife to have an outside job?
3. If your husband were against your having a job, what would you do?
4. If you had young children, would you give up your job, at least temporarily?
5. Do you think a career woman has more likelihood of divorce?
6. Do you think women are discriminated against in the job market, especially if they are pregnant?
7. Is it true that stay-at-home moms are looked down at in society compared with career women? Why or why not?

Opinion Samples

1. I'm angry because mothers who stay home are looked down upon, while working moms are praised and respected. I know too many working mothers who live in luxurious homes, have a BMW in the driveway and a swimming pool in the backyard, and take European vacations. Meanwhile, they're paying strangers to look after their kids. Let's get back to raising our own families, wearing less expensive clothes, driving economical cars, and doing what women were meant to do — being homemakers and full-time mothers.

I wouldn't dream of giving the responsibility and fun of raising my children to anyone else. It's the most fulfilling and rewarding job in the world.

(Q) Which role is more important for women — raising children or making money?

2. In my opinion, wives should manage to live on what their husbands earn, because a career woman is potentially a good candidate[↓] for divorce. When a woman becomes financially independent, she neglects her husband and children, and her marriage falls apart. Marriages were much healthier when women stayed home and took care of their husbands and raised their own kids.

(Q) Do you think the speaker is old-fashioned? Or an accurate observer of humankind?

3. The days when men controlled women by keeping them poor, pregnant, and barefoot are gone forever. If a woman chooses to stay home and live on what her husband can provide, fine. But today, because more women can support themselves, they have a choice.

(Q) Would you be willing to respect your wife's decision to work outside the home? Why or why not?

4. I'm tired—not just "tired," but bone-weary[↓] exhausted. I'm the female of the New Millennium, a professional woman with a good husband and three wonderful children. I put in 40 hours a week downtown and just as many at home. When people like me are written up in a women's magazine or a newspaper article, you'd think we had the world by the tail.[↓] Baloney.[↓]

My job as a supervisor is stressful. The demands on me are awesome. Everyone wants something. And when I come home I must prepare supper, clean the house, wash clothes, pick up the kids from school or other activities, help them with homework, and see that they are bathed and put to bed. By then I'm totally shot.[↓] My body says rest, but my mind says I must get ready for tomorrow.

- **candidate :** person deserving of a certain fate
- **bone-weary :** completely tired
- **have the world by the tail :** be in a controlling position
- **baloney :** nonsense
- **shot :** exhausted

I'm 45 pounds overweight, and every week I add another pound or two. This is another area of my life that I can't seem to control. I know I should go on a diet, but I don't feel like tackling another big job right now.

My husband helps more than most husbands, and the children are our top priority. I truly wish I didn't have to work, but there is no way we could make it financially if I stayed home. I'm not working so we can have a Mercedes, a pool, or a fancy vacation. I work so we can meet our house and car payments, buy decent clothes and put food on the table. We are not extravagant people. Even though my husband and I are both professionals, we don't make a great deal of money. If I quit work it would cut our income in half.

My parents live across town. They are retired and depend on me a lot. This is another heavy burden. They were terrific parents. I feel guilty that I can't do more for them.

(Q) What do you think women work for? For money? For success? For what?

- **tackle :** take on and wrestle with (an opponent or a problem, for ex.)
- **fancy :** of superior grade; fine
- **extravagant :** tending to spend money lavishly or inappropriately

Issue 17

A Marriage Between the Haves and Have-nots

My husband's family had nothing. My family was prominent in social and financial circles. He said we were from different worlds, but I assured him our love could bridge the gap. I was willing to live on his salary, which meant doing without many things I'd become accustomed to. Our troubles began on our honeymoon. He accused my parents of putting on a ridiculously lavish wedding to flaunt their wealth and said his family felt out of place. His needling continued until it became intolerable. He'd look at me and say, "You miss going out shopping all the time, don't you?" "No," I would insist, and he'd call me a liar and I'd end up in tears. This sort of cruelty went on for two years. Finally I got so thin and nervous, I knew that if I didn't leave him I'd have a complete breakdown. When I packed and went home, he told everyone who'd ask, "She couldn't take it. I just wasn't

- **prominent :** well-known; eminent
- **circle :** sphere; realm
- **bridge the gap :** reduce the difference
- **do without :** forego; dispense with
- **lavish :** extravagant, overly expensive
- **flaunt :** show off (sth) with too much pride
- **out of place :** unsuitable; inappropriate
- **needle :** provoke
- **breakdown :** the condition of failing to function properly

able to make enough money to keep her satisfied." I want to let people know that a marriage between the haves and have-nots can be a terrible uphill fight, but not for the reasons most people imagine. Sometimes, there is a perverse pleasure in poverty that engenders its own form of snobbery.

What Does It Mean?

1. doing without many things I'd become accustomed to
2. perverse pleasure

Comprehension

1. What did the man complain about on his honeymoon?
2. What did he say when she left?

- **uphill :** very tiring or difficult
- **perverse :** stubbornly opposing or resisting what is right, expected, or reasonable
- **engender :** cause a feeling or attitude to exist
- **snobbery :** the attitudes and behavior of (sb) who admires or behaves like people of the higher social ranks

Let's Talk!

1. What was the problem between this couple?
2. What problems might the following differences cause between spouses?
   (a) in education
   (b) in religion
   (c) in character
   (d) in family background
   (e) in social status
   (f) in attitudes toward life
3. Which is the hardest to overcome among the above differences?
4. Which is the easiest ?
5. What is the most important way to cope for couples with many differences?

Opinion Samples

1. When I was in high school our class read a play by Thornton Wilder called "Our Town." What I most remember is one of the characters wondering what married couples talked about all their lives, and how they kept from running out of new topics. This still seems important to me today, as I contemplate marriage. I'm convinced more than ever that educational differences must be minimal for a marriage to work. An intelligent, inquisitive wife (or husband, for that matter) would soon be bored stiff by the limited curiosity of a dull spouse, in the same way that the slug spouse would grow tired of the uninteresting, self-centered conversation of the other. They both need to be on the same level if they even hope to be able to talk to each other every day over several decades.

(Q) What if your would-be spouse came from a very different background — how could the two of you bridge the gap?

2. Opposites may attract, but they don't make for easy companions. Someone who enjoys reading a good book may not want to forego that pleasure to take a long hike in the mountains, and the mountaineer probably wouldn't be happy staying quietly at home all day. A hard-nosed pessimist may get tired of hearing the spouse's unrelentingly foolish optimism. Some people want to hold in their feelings and deal with a situation stoically without engaging in histrionic complaint, and others think the only way to solve a problem is to air their differences completely and energetically.

(Q) Who do you think would have a happier marriage, a couple who have the same life philosophy or one with radically different attitudes?

- **minimal :** smallest in amount or degree
- **inquisitive :** curious
- **bored stiff :** very uninterested
- **slug :** lazy, idle person
- **forego :** give up (sth)
- **hard-nosed :** uncompromising; tough
- **unrelenting :** unstoppable; not quitting
- **stoical :** accepting things without complaining
- **histrionic :** expressing very strong feelings; over-reacting emotionally
- **air :** say (sth) publicly; display

Issue 18

Panhandling

This is my experience with a "homeless" man carrying a large "Will Work for Food" sign: He was living in the bushes behind my husband's place of employment. When police arrested him for trespassing and vagrancy, they found $1,000 in cash in his pockets. He told the police he had made the money by standing at a busy intersection in town with one of those signs. He also said he could never do as well working, because he takes in $500 to $600 a day just holding up that sign. Think about this: If one person gave you a dollar every time the car had to stop, and the signal changed 30 times an hour, and you stood there for eight hours a day, you could make $240 a day. Realistically, the figures are probably much higher. I recently saw a family (a mother, a father, and three young children) standing at a busy intersection holding these "homeless" signs. Not only is this activity dangerous, it's also emotional blackmail.

- **panhandle :** beg for money on the street or in a public area
- **trespass :** go on the property of another without permission
- **vagrancy :** not having a settled life or regular occupation
- **intersection :** place where two or more roads cross
- **figure :** amount or value expressed in numbers
- **blackmail :** act of frightening or embarrassing (sb) into making a payment of money

What Does It Mean?

1. He also said he could never do as well working.
2. Realistically, the figures are probably much higher.
3. emotional blackmail

Comprehension

1. Why was the man with the "Will Work for Food" sign arrested?
2. What did the police find in his pocket?
3. How did he make the money?
4. How much does he probably make a day?
5. What does the writer think about this kind of panhandling?

Let's Talk!

1. Do you usually give beggars money? Why or why not?
2. How much do you usually give them?
3. Do you feel guilty when you give panhandlers nothing? Why or why not?
4. Do you agree that panhandling is emotional blackmail? Explain your answer.
5. Many people say that when you give money to panhandlers, it only encourages them to beg more. What do you think of the theory?
6. Do you think it is fair that beggars may make much more money than ordinary salaried workers?
7. Do you think the government should permit panhandling?
8. Talk about ways of preventing panhandling on the street.
9. What would you think about making panhandling a formal job classification and taxing it?
10. Panhandling entails no taxes or hard work, and has flexible hours. What would you think about doing this as your permanent job?
11. What do you think about street vendors? Should we legalize and tax them? What would the side effects be?

Opinion Samples

1. I think we have no moral obligation to give anything to panhandlers if begging is a very lucrative business and they generally make much more money than average people do. Do you think it fair that relatively poor people should give money to the rich?

(Q) Do you think panhandlers really do make more money than ordinary people?

2. The government shouldn't allow panhandlers on the street. They cause people anxiety over whether to give something or not. Some people feel guilty when they don't give them money. That's why I think panhandling is emotional blackmail.

(Q) Would you ban all kinds of panhandling, no types, or only some? If the latter, which ones?

→ **lucrative :** producing wealth; profitable
→ **average :** typical kind, or usual level or degree

Issue 19

Platonic Friends

[A]

My husband and I are trying to put our marriage back together after his affair with another woman. We've been in counseling and learned a great deal about ourselves and each other. I believe him when he says he wants to stay with me and work things out. I also believe that he has been faithful since we started counseling. There is one sticking point, however. He insists that I accept this other woman as his "friend," someone with whom he can share his work and intellectual interests. The friend has had more formal education than I, but I am not a dummy.

Their friendship consists of phone calls, letters, and an occasional drink. I know he continues to share personal information about our marriage with this woman and she "advises" him. I can't believe that her input is unbiased, nor do I believe that her own needs and desires don't affect her judgment.

I must add that I have never cared whether or not my husband's friends were male or female. He has other female friends, which is OK with me because I don't feel they are a threat to our marriage. I'm unable to be impartial toward this woman, however, because she tried to break up our home and hurt our children.

[B]

I am a 44-year-old woman who is having a platonic relationship with a 35-year-old man. There is nothing sexual involved—we just have lunch together and maybe see a movie every few weeks. My husband just began to grumble about our relationship and ordered me to knock off those lunches and movies. But I think I am an adult who is free to have lunch with any friend I choose, regardless of age, sex, race, creed, or marital status.

- **affair :** brief romantic relationship
- **sticking :** not smooth or easy; difficult
- **dummy :** stupid or foolish person
- **consist of :** be made of
- **grumble :** complain in a rude or unfriendly manner; mutter unhappily
- **knock off :** stop (sth)
- **creed :** system of belief or principles that guides a person's actions
- **marital status :** condition of being single, married, separated, or divorced

[C]

I'm a 27-year-old single woman living in a fairly small town. I've worked with a married man for five years, and I would say we were good friends. He suggested that we meet in another town, have a few drinks and get a hotel room. I was offended, walked away, and refused to speak to him for three weeks. He's 42 and has three children.

I started talking to him again, and he hasn't harassed me in any way. He's well-respected in the community, and I've told no one about his suggestion. I really like him a lot, but I would never forgive myself if I were to become sexually involved with a married man. If he had just suggested the drinks and not the hotel room, I might have accepted. I would like to know him better, and there aren't many opportunities to talk at work.

Is it OK for us to become closer friends and maintain a platonic relationship? I don't want to hurt his marriage or his reputation, but I'd like to know him better intellectually (not physically). I could learn a lot from him. We have not discussed his suggestion since I turned him down. Should I bring it up and make my feelings clear to him?

What Does It Mean?

QUES...

1. put our marriage back together
2. sticking point
3. I am not a dummy.
4. She "advises" him.
5. I can't believe that her input is unbiased, nor do I believe that her own needs and desires don't affect her judgment.
6. unable to be impartial
7. platonic relationship
8. I was offended.

- **fairly :** to some degree, but not completely or extremely
- **turn (sb/sth) down :** reject or refuse (a person, advice, or a suggestion)

Comprehension

[A] 1. What is getting in the way of the couple putting their marriage back together?
2. Do the husband and his "girlfriend" enjoy their relationship?
3. Why does the wife feel OK about her husband's other female friends?
4. Why does the wife worry about this particular woman?

[B] 1. How old is the woman's friend?
2. What do they do when they see each other?
3. Does her husband accept the relationship?
4. Why does she think she has a right to have a relationship with anyone she chooses?

[C] 1. How long has she worked with the married man?
2. What did he suggest recently?
3. Why did she refuse his suggestion?
4. Did he continue to rub her the wrong way after she rejected his suggestion?
5. Why does she want to know him better?

Let's Talk!

1. Is it possible for a man to see a woman as a friend after they have had a love affair?
2. Is friendship or a platonic (nonsexual) relationship possible between a man and a woman?
3. If your spouse had a close platonic relationship with a person of the opposite sex, could you accept it?
4. Would it be more acceptable if the relationship were open or secretive?
5. Have you ever had a platonic relationship with someone of the opposite sex?
6. Do you think that common interests, hobbies, work, or intellectual pursuits would be a good enough reason for a platonic relationship?
7. Do you think either a husband or a wife has a right to "order" the end to a platonic relationship of the spouse?
8. What is your definition of platonic friendship?

→ rub (sb) the wrong way : do or say things that annoy (sb)

Opinion Samples

1. They talk on the phone, write letters, and meet occasionally to have a drink, and he wants to call it platonic? Nonsense. I don't buy that.

(Q) Do you think such apparently harmless activities comprise something more than a relationship between just friends?

2. Her husband needs to grow up. The relationship is not secret, and she says there is nothing sexual about it. I think her husband has nothing to worry about. What we would really have to worry about is a secret relationship, which inevitably entails sexual wrong-doing.

(Q) Do you think there is nothing to worry about if the relationship is open?

3. When one of the spouses has a so-called "platonic relationship," it's a dynamite situation which will eventually explode. Married men and women don't "date" other people. If they value their marriage, they should stop the relationship immediately. The situation might start out very innocently, but end up in a motel room.

(Q) So, is it impossible to have a close friend of the opposite sex if one is married?

- **buy :** accept or believe
- **comprise :** consist of; include
- **entail :** cause or involve by necessity or as a consequence

Issue 20

Marrying Young

Let me tell you what it is like to be a married girl at 19. It's coming home so tired you feel nearly dead. But you don't dare sit down because you might never get up. And there are still so many things you have to do. The cooking, the washing, the ironing. But you go through the motions nonetheless, because you have to. You hate your job. You ask yourself, "Why don't you quit?" And you know why. Because there are grocery bills and medical bills and the rent to pay. And your young hubby's crummy little check won't cover them. That's why.

Then you have to play with the baby. Only sometimes you don't feel like it. But you do it anyway. Because you feel guilty about being away from her all day. Then you mix the formula and change diapers.

When your husband doesn't come home, you know he has decided to go out with the boys again. Or, you pray it is only "the boys" he is with. So, finally, you eat the lousy meal by yourself and go to bed and cry your eyes out.

When he does come home, you can tell he's been drinking. But you don't say a word because he hates to be told anything. So you try to sleep so you can dream about the good old days. You think about the great meals your mother used to cook, and how nice your room was at home.

Then you remember how she tried to talk you out of marrying so young, and how you got mad at her and called her a dried-up old woman who forgot what it was like to be in love.

And you try to push the

- crummy : of poor quality; miserable
- formula : liquid food for infants, containing many of the nutrients in human milk
- lousy : of low quality; very bad
- dried-up : spoiled with age, lacking vital juices

thoughts of other boys out of your mind, but those thoughts keep coming back. Especially that certain boy who gave you your first kiss. He won the science prize at school and is going to be a doctor. You wonder how different your life would have been if you had married him instead, or if you had gone to college.

You have the feeling that the husband you chose and the baby and the life you lead are all part of a bad dream. But you know it's no dream. It's for real. You cry yourself to sleep and wake up with a splitting headache in the morning.

What Does It Mean?

1. go through the motions
2. feel guilty about being away from her all day
3. You pray it is only "the boys" he is with.

Comprehension

1. What is it like for her to have married so young?
2. Why does she have to keep her job?
3. Was her mother in favor of the early marriage?
4. Why didn't she follow her mom's advice? (Give more than one answer, based on the reading itself.)

→ splitting : painful; intense; severe

Let's Talk!

1. Which do you think is worse, marrying too young or marrying too late?
2. What are the advantages and disadvantages of marrying young?
3. What are the advantages and disadvantages of marrying late in life?
4. What do young people think love is?
5. What do older people think about love?
6. What are some common mistakes young people make when they are in love?
7. What determines a happy marriage? Is it one thing, or a combination of things?
8. What is your definition of love?
9. What is the relationship between love and marriage?

Opinion Samples

1. Love is a virulent epidemic that affects our ability to think like rational human beings. It makes us behave like giddy children or drug addicts. Our vision is affected in such a way that we cannot even see the real person we are in love with. Bad behavior on his or her part is automatically excused or rationalized away, character faults disappear, and physical shortcomings are trivialized. The only thing that matters is how much of ourselves we are able to sacrifice on behalf of the loved one. Every word and gesture he or she makes, every attitude he or she expresses, every thought or whim becomes a sign that must be interpreted and incorporated into our world. Neither age nor station, nor history nor philosophy, presents an effective vaccine against the love virus. No one is immune. Not even you.

(Q) What could be a vaccine for blind love?

- **virulent :** extremely infectious, malignant, or poisonous; very harsh or bitter
- **epidemic :** serious, widespread disease
- **giddy :** silly and not interested in serious things
- **rationalize :** invent seemingly satisfactory but false explanations for (sb's) behavior
- **fault :** defect
- **shortcoming :** flaw
- **trivialized :** made to seem smaller or less important
- **whim :** sudden or unimportant idea or desire
- **station :** position in society

2. Perhaps love is a form of worship (whether mutual or one-sided), and marriage is a manifestation of pragmatic necessity. Marriage is part of every human society, though it takes many forms and performs many functions. It defines status and identity, unites or divides property, and lays a basis for the offspring's place in the world and thus perpetuates or interrupts a family line. It establishes a factory where all manner of work is accomplished: sex, companionship, parenthood, affection, wardrobe maintenance, physical sustenance. Love may or may not be integral to marriage. Many loveless marriages have been eminently successful, just as many love matches have proved disastrous. Some married couples have learned to love each other over time, some have lost their early affection for each other, some have become indifferent or hateful toward their partner. The popular idea still associates love with marriage, but in actual fact, perhaps the two institutions have little to do with each other in most cases.

(Q) Which do you think would be better, a loveless marriage with money or a love marriage with no money?

- **manifestation :** the showing or proving of (sth)
- **perpetuate :** cause (sth) to continue indefinitely
- **interrupt :** cause (sth) to stop, usually temporarily
- **wardrobe :** the clothes that someone has
- **sustenance :** nourishment
- **integral :** necessary to form a whole
- **eminently :** completely and without a doubt
- **associate :** connect

Issue 21

Be

– Be understanding to your enemies.
– Be loyal to your friends.
– Be strong enough to face the world each day.
– Be weak enough to know you cannot do everything alone.
– Be generous to those who need your help.
– Be frugal with what you need yourself.
– Be wise enough to know that you do not know everything.
– Be foolish enough to believe in miracles.
– Be willing to share your joys.
– Be willing to share the sorrows of others.
– Be a leader when you are sure of the correct action.
– Be a follower when you are shrouded by the mists of uncertainty.
– Be the first to congratulate an opponent who succeeds.
– Be the last to criticize a colleague who fails.
– Be sure where to place your next step, so you will not stumble.
– Be loving to those who love you.
– Be loving to those who do not love you, and they may change.
– Above all, be yourself.

- shrouded : covered
- colleague : fellow member of a profession, staff, or organization; associate
- stumble : walk in an unsteady way, almost falling

What Does It Mean?

1. foolish enough to believe in miracles
2. shrouded by the mists of uncertainty
3. be yourself

Comprehension

1. Why should you be careful where you walk?
2. How strong should we be?
3. What might happen if we love someone who doesn't love us?

Let's Talk!

1. Are you capable of being generous to your enemies? Discuss the matter in detail.
2. In what ways are you loyal to your friends?
3. What's the difference between being frugal and being cheap?
4. Do you believe in miracles? Why or why not?
5. With whom can you share your joys?
6. With whom do you share your sorrows?
7. Why is it hard to congratulate an opponent for his success?
8. Is it easy to be loving towards those who do not love you? Do you think they will change their attitude towards you?

Opinion Samples

1. No one is perfect. We all lose our tempers or speak before we think. Sometimes we act in a rude, disgusting manner. We are most likely to behave this way when our guard is down because we are with people who know us well. But our real friends will excuse our temporary lapse of civility and continue to be our friends, and of course we have the same obligation for tolerance toward them. On the other hand, continuous, repeated bad treatment by so-called friends probably indicates a genuine lack of friendship on their part, and the association deserves to be reexamined. Like all social relationships, friendship is reciprocal, needing

- **cheap :** not spending or giving money; stingy
- **lose (one's) temper :** suddenly become angry and lose control of (one's) behavior
- **disgusting :** extremely unpleasant
- **guard is down :** relaxed, unconcerned about danger
- **lapse :** slip or failure, esp. a minor one
- **association :** relationship
- **reciprocal :** given or owed to each other; treated mutually

both behavioral input and output to sustain itself. Loyalty is an integral part of the constitution; a "disloyal friend" is a contradiction in terms.

(Q) What do you really mean by "true" friend? What do you really want from your friends?

2. Are you thrifty? Is your neighbor miserly? You both behave in a similar way: you avoid spending money foolishly and believe that saving money is a noble act. "A penny saved is a penny earned," as Ben Franklin expressed it. So, what is the difference? The answer is one of perspective, only; when we want to praise someone's frugality, we use adjectives with a positive connotation, and when we wish to condemn the identical attitude, we use adjectives with negative spin. The behavior being described is objectively the same, but our relationship to the perpetrator is different. (The same is true, of course, for the opposite action as well: emotional coloration is the only difference between being generous and being a spendthrift.)

(Q) List the behavioral characteristics of being frugal and being a cheapskate.

- thrift : careful management of money and other resources
- miserly : reluctant to spend money
- frugal : careful in spending or in using resources
- spin : way of giving information; angle
- perpetrator : (sb) who does (sth) wrong
- spendthrift : (sb) who spends money wastefully or foolishly
- cheapskate : insulting word for (sb) thought to be stingy

Issue 22

The New Work Regimen

I work for a big company and have a terrific job. After it downsized, however, I now work 60-hour-plus weeks. I do the same job four other people used to do. By the time I get home, I'm thoroughly exhausted. But, nevertheless, I take a ton of work home with me and spend several hours a night on the phone or checking my electronic mail on my computer at home.

Of course, I am quite thankful for my job, which has provided me with an interesting career and a comfortable lifestyle for many years, and I don't consider myself a whiner. But the new pace and the hours I have to keep are absurd. It burdens not only myself but my family as well. What is worse, the company refuses to see that this regimen will have negative long-term effects upon itself.

When you work constantly, your mind doesn't function as well as it normally does. I know I am not as productive on the job as I should be. Because I'm tired, I don't take the same pride in my work I used to, so slap-dash is good enough for me these days. I don't have any opportunity to spend my money enjoyably, so I don't much care how much I make, and I don't have any incentive at all to work harder to

- downsize : become smaller, esp. to reduce costs in a company or organization
- ton of : lot of
- whine : complain in a sad, annoying voice about (sth)
- slap-dash : doing (sth) quickly and not carefully
- incentive : (sth) that encourages action or effort

make more. So, the company is suffering as well.

This is not just my opinion. I hear this from friends and coworkers, too. It seems to me that if the work we do can't be done in a normal work week, then perhaps we need more people to do the job. Or we need less work to do.

What Does It Mean?

1. downsized
2. the pace and hours are absurd

Comprehension

1. What happened to the job after the company downsized?
2. Why doesn't the person work as productively as before?
3. Why should more people be hired?

Let's Talk!

1. What will probably happen if these work conditions go unabated?
2. Would you continue to work under these circumstances, or would you quit?
3. Is there a work style that would suit the needs of managers and employees alike? If so, describe it.
4. Would you work extra hours for better pay?
5. Who do you think do the most work, employees or employers?
6. Who do you think is more responsible if a company is in trouble —workers or bosses?

Opinion Samples

1. "Work" is not a very adequate word. Too many people think that the only workers are the ones who use their hands to make something or extract something; even the notion of typing or filing something is not always accorded the status of work by those who discount "white collar" jobs as somehow bogus. This ignores the simple fact that work also includes brain work. Sellers, organizers, strategists and others keep the workplace alive. If they fail, the manual workers have nothing to do and soon have no job either. If one measures work in terms of time spent on the job, the people who perform the mental functions usually put in the longest days and weeks. Everyone else can go home at the end of the shift, but the non-physical workers never truly finish the job and have to be available at any hour. It is like the human body. The muscles may be strong and flexible, the organs may all perform their tasks to perfection, but if the brain goes dead, everything else collapses as well.

(Q) Which people want to be white-collar workers and which blue-collar workers? Who are better paid? Why?

- **unabated :** unable to be stopped or controlled
- **accord :** grant
- **bogus :** not true or real
- **shift :** person's scheduled period of work
- **collapse :** break down or fail suddenly and completely

2. Whose responsibility is it for a company's success?

(a) It depends. If the company is in trouble, workers are naturally expected to sacrifice their time and money until the situation improves. If it is doing well, the executives need to reward their workers for their productivity.

(b) Nobody can have a job without having problems. But one thing is clear, everybody feels overworked and under-appreciated.

(c) Look for a job that is not very demanding, even though it may mean a smaller paycheck. Money isn't everything. I've never heard of a man on his deathbed saying, "I wish I could have spent more time at the office."

(Q) Discuss the answer in light of the attitudes above?

Issue 23

Two Sides of the Same Coin

Many an unfortunate marriage could have been avoided if the two parties had discussed frankly, in advance, what each one wanted. Here is an example:

"My husband won't be satisfied until he has all the money in the world. He works 16 hours a day. He's a stranger to his children, and I may as well be a widow for all I see of him. This beautiful home we live in doesn't mean a thing. I'd rather have just one room and share it with an attentive husband."

The other side of the coin can look just as bad:

"The problem with my other half is that he has no ambition. He could add 40 percent to his income if he'd only work Saturdays and a few evenings a week. But no, he'd rather take the kids fishing or watch TV with me, or putter around the house fixing something that isn't really broken. I tell him there's more to being a husband and father than just spending time with us. In fact, being a constant companion is the most selfish

- attentive : marked by careful attention to the comfort of others; considerate
- putter : do (sth) in an aimless or ineffective manner

aspect of the roles. I'm sure he gets a lot of personal satisfaction, but if he had any gumption he'd earn a little more money so the girls could have decent clothes and the boys could have a new bike, and we could all live in a nicer home. Our kids will never go to college unless they put themselves through. We haven't got more than two cents to our name."

What Does It Mean?

1. This beautiful home we live in doesn't mean a thing.
2. We haven't got more than two cents to our name.

Comprehension

1. What does the first wife want her husband to do?
2. What does the second one want her hubby to do?
3. How could both situations have been avoided in advance?

- **gumption :** boldness, courage, or spirit
- **decent :** adequate; passable
- **put (sb) through school/college :** pay for (sb) to get an education

Let's Talk!

1. What is wrong with working hard to provide one's family with a better life?
2. How can it be wrong to spend as much time as possible with one's family?
3. How can one establish a suitable balance between work and family?
4. Which wife do you agree with most, the first or second? Defend her attitude.
5. Does money play an affirmative or negative role in your life?

Opinion Samples

1. No one can get by without money; and the more one has, the easier it is to get by. Nice, comfortable homes, safe cars, travel and relaxation, health care, education—all are expensive. The repercussions of poverty, even relative poverty, extend beyond one's own lifetime into far distant generations. Don't you think it would be tragic to shortchange your family merely because you lacked the money to get the best available?

People often talk about how corrupting great wealth is to moral and social obligations. But corruption is entirely an individual matter; poor people may be just as evil and apathetic as rich ones; indeed, the lack of sufficient resources may impel the poor to cheat, steal, lie, kill, merely to survive, while the wealthy may do those things on a mere whim. The responsible rich will behave in an acceptable manner, but the responsible poor may not have that option in every instance.

(Q) Is there any inconvenience in being rich or any good point about poverty?

- **repercussion :** indirect effect or result of an event or action
- **shortchange :** treat (sb) unfairly by not giving what is deserved
- **corrupt :** ruin (sb) morally; destroy the honesty of (sb)
- **apathetic :** indifferent
- **impel :** urge (sb) to action; drive

2. A solid marriage is based on reality. Dream castles in the sky may be lovely to think about, but don't try to live in one. You'll come crashing through the vapory floor until you are grounded (fatally) on the truth. So, before you get married, you need to do some thinking, deep and serious. What spousal values are important to you for maintaining family life? Financial stability, social status, celebrity, religion, sexual fidelity, generosity, artistic sensibility, beauty, athleticism? An affectionate nature, or a money-making ambition? An old name or a new start? Make a mental list, be as exclusive and exact as possible, and then try to apply these criteria as ruthlessly as a computer dating game. But don't be surprised if your program has not been thoroughly debugged; you may end up attached to a completely different kind of program. And, maybe, you'll even be better off!

(Q) What do you expect from your future spouse?

- **an old name :** a distinguished family
- **a new start :** beginning from scratch
- **exclusive :** limited to narrow criteria
- **ruthless :** without pity or compassion
- **debug :** search for and fix errors

Issue 24

Before You Kill Yourself

You've decided to do it. Life is impossible. Suicide is your only way out. Fine! But before you finalize your decision, there are some things you should know. Suicide is usually not successful. You think you know a guaranteed method? Ask the 25-year-old who tried to electrocute himself. He lived. But both his arms are gone.

What about jumping? Ask John. He used to be intelligent, with an engaging sense of humor. That was before he leaped from an apartment building. Now he's brain-damaged and will always need care. He staggers and has seizures. He lives in a fog. But worst of all, he still knows he used to be normal.

What about pills? Ask the 12-year-old with extensive liver damage caused by an overdose. Have you ever seen anyone die of liver damage? First you turn yellow, all over your body. Then you waste away, getting weaker week by week. It's effective but is at best suicide in slow motion.

What about using a gun? Ask the man who shot himself in the head. Today he drags one leg, has a useless arm and no vision or hearing on one side. Unfortunately, he lived through his "foolproof" suicide method. You might, too.

Suicide is also contagious. Look around at your family. Look closely at the 4-year-old playing with his cars on the rug. Kill yourself tonight, and he may do it 10 years from now. His sister may do it the year after. And the

- finalize : put (sth) into final form; complete
- electrocute : kill or execute (sb) with electricity
- engaging : having attraction
- stagger : move or stand unsteadily
- seizure : sudden attack, as of some mental or physical disorder
- extensive : wide; broad; large
- waste away : gradually become thinner and weaker
- contagious : tending to spread from person to person

ever-so-carefully worded "loving" suicide note is no help. Because those who loved you will never completely recover. They'll not only feel regret and an unending pain, but the burden of guilt as well.

You do have other choices, though. There are people who can help you through this crisis. Call a hot line. Call a friend or relative. Call your minister or priest. Call a doctor or a hospital. Call the police. They will all tell you that there is hope.

What Does It Mean?

1. a way to guarantee it
2. Suicide is contagious.
3. "loving" suicide note
4. Those who loved you will never completely recover.

Comprehension

1. Is suicide usually successful?
2. How many ways of killing oneself are mentioned?
3. What would happen to the suicide's family?
4. If someone is toying with thoughts of suicide, how many options does he have, according to the essay? Can you think of any others?

→ **hot line :** telephone number for emergency counseling
→ **toy with :** think about an idea or possibility, usually for a short time and not very seriously

Let's Talk!

1. Have you ever felt an impulse to kill yourself? If so, when and why? Did you succeed?
2. Talk about reasons people may have to commit suicide.
3. Do you think a man has the right to control his own life, including the decision to end it?
4. There are many people who have thought about committing suicide but didn't go through with it. Why not, in your judgment?
5. Is life always better than death in any case? Why or why not?
6. Who do you think are the most likely to kill themselves: the young, the middle-aged or the elderly? Why?

Opinion Samples

1. The question of free will has long bedeviled mankind. Does it exist—does a person choose the ways in which his life is led, or are they predetermined by God, genes, Fate, psychology, the environment, economics, society, or some other factor? But, surely, every individual holds at least one arrow in his quiver. He may not know how long his life CAN last, but he definitely can bring it to a close whenever he chooses.

Such a decision should not be taken lightly, of course—it is a card that can only be played once and no more. But no conscious person should have to endure insufferable pain, or subject his family to the awesome consequences, financial and psychological, of a long terminal illness. If it is

- **bedevil :** trouble in a mean way
- **gene :** basic physical unit of heredity
- **quiver :** case for holding or carrying arrows
- **insufferable :** difficult or impossible to endure
- **subject :** cause (sb) or (sth) to undergo or experience (sth)

absolutely certain that death is near in any case, why not go out at a time and in a manner that you choose? Perhaps stage a massive celebration of your life and accomplishments, invite all your friends and relatives, resolve any unsettled scores among yourselves, indulge yourself to the fullest extent possible, and then, after you have said your last good-byes to everyone important in your life, ingest some peacefully fatal potion and end it all? Isn't this better than having your loved ones remember mainly how you lived in pain and delirium, how your mind dimmed and your body shriveled over the final weeks or months of your life?

(Q) What do you want your last moment to be?

2. Life is always better than death. In life, there is hope, even when the situation is the most hopeless. Miracles can and do occur. Endurance and the refusal to surrender mark a character of the highest order. But death is the Great Finality from which no change can occur. Death transcends, in a negative way, all that is valuable in life. Giving in needlessly to death is the height of cowardice. Pain may be a terrible master, but less ignominious than shame. When Death taps you on the shoulder, spit in his face. Shout, "Do your damnest!" as you blacken his eye and break his nose. You may lose—but at least you'll go down fighting.

(Q) Why should anyone fight if he knows he will lose?

- **score :** difficulty, dispute
- **indulge :** yield to the wishes of (sb)
- **ingest :** take into the body, as food or liquid
- **potion :** liquid dose, esp. of medicine or poison
- **delirium :** temporary state of confusion resulting from high fever, poisoning, or shock
- **dim :** become less bright
- **shrivel :** become shrunken or wrinkled
- **transcend :** go beyond (sth)
- **give in :** surrender; yield
- **cowardice :** lack of courage, or a shameful show of fear, when facing danger or pain
- **ignominious :** characterized by shame or embarrassment; humiliating
- **do your damnest :** try your hardest to hurt me (indicating a lack of fear)
- **blacken :** become black or make (sth) black
- **go down :** be prepared to start doing (sth)

Issue 25

The Real Person

A real person is one who manages to be himself. This sounds elementary, and perhaps even naive, but don't be fooled. Being yourself is a challenging task because first you need to know yourself. And few people do.

What are you really like? Would you be offended if I were to suggest that you are two people? (Well, after all, everyone is.) First you are the self with many unattractive qualities: the secret desires, the large and small fears, the nagging insecurities, the twinges of envy, of cowardice, of avarice. Second is the self you proudly present to the world: courageous, confident, mature, selfless. This is the self each of us wants the world to see.

It is impossible to be 100 percent real. The society we live in, whatever society that may be, requires us to pretend to behave in a certain prescribed manner, even though it may be contrary to our own desire. But the better adjusted we are, the more genuine we become.

So, a genuine person has a consistency which runs through every phase of his interpersonal relationships. Manners are not relative. He doesn't shower someone with attention one day and ignore him the next. He doesn't wear one face for the CEO and another for the janitor. He doesn't smile sweetly to his dinner partner and then, within seconds, bark orders to the waiter. He operates at a high ethical level and within a predictable framework. His responses to trying situations are disciplined and civilized. He doesn't switch positions, abandon his principles, or change his personality to fit his mood, the company, the weather, or the state of his digestion.

- **offend :** cause (sb) to become angry
- **nag :** bother endlessly
- **twinge :** mental or emotional pain
- **avarice :** extreme desire for money or wealth; greed
- **shower (sb) with (sth) :** give a large number of (sth) to (sb)
- **janitor :** one whose job is to clean and take care of a building

A "real" person uses a simple conversational alphabet. There is no capital "I" and no small "u." He is not driven to exaggerate his virtues or his achievements. He doesn't pretend to be wealthier, wiser, better (or worse) than he really is. He doesn't try to overwhelm others by name-dropping or place-dropping. The man who brags about his family tree reveals himself as the sap. And we all know people who select their church, politics, and clubs solely on the basis of what the affiliation might do for them socially or financially.

What Does It Mean?

1. don't be fooled
2. prescribed manner
3. There is no capital "I" and no small "u."
4. The man who brags about his family tree reveals himself as the sap.

Comprehension

1. Who are the two people in ourselves?
2. What does "consistency" mean in terms of a real person?
3. By what criteria would a real person choose a church, political party, or club to belong to? How do most people decide?

- **exaggerate :** speak or write about (sth) as if it is greater or more important than it is
- **virtue :** moral goodness
- **name-drop :** mention the names of famous or important people in order to impress (sb)
- **place-drop :** mention places one has been in order to impress (sb)
- **sap :** foolish person
- **affiliation :** connection with an organization, esp. a political or religious one

Let's Talk!

1. What are some of the manners society prescribes for us? Be specific.
2. Do you think the traditionally prescribed manners are always the right ones? Why or why not?
3. Are there any prescribed manners that are contrary to your own desires?
4. By what criteria would you choose a college to attend? What about choosing a college for your children?
5. By what criteria do you choose your friends?
6. By what criteria did you choose your religion?
7. By what criteria would you choose your job?

Opinion Samples

1. Manners are culturally transmitted, and so sometimes a gracious gesture is misconstrued as being rude in a different situation. Arabs are well-known for wanting to be in very close proximity to each other when they talk, but Americans feel uncomfortable unless there is a lot of space between them. For the English, most people they deal with on a daily basis are known by their titles (Mr. Jones, for instance) even if they have known them for years, but Australians prefer to be known immediately by their first names and expect to address everyone else the same way. Notoriously, it is said that Eskimo men believe that it is the epitome of civility to loan their wives to a visiting stranger for the night, but most other peoples would regard the practice as barbaric.

(Q) Are there any traditional manners you want to throw away?

- **gracious :** pleasantly kind; wishing well to others; courteous
- **misconstrue :** misunderstand; misinterpret
- **proximity :** state, quality of being near; closeness
- **epitome :** typical example of an entire class or type
- **barbaric :** crude or uncivilized

2. One custom that has always bothered me about the Asian societies I have known is their high degree of hypocrisy. Of course, everyone is two-faced to some extent; we all find it easier to be polite than insulting, especially if we are trying to impress somebody or avoid an argument, or if we don't want to hurt someone's feelings needlessly. But as a Westerner, I find the Eastern habit of avoidance behavior unsettling. People tell me they are going to do something and then do the opposite. Or knowing that they are going to do something that concerns me directly, they do not tell me about it, so I find myself unpleasantly surprised when it finally happens. I have had friends who were seriously dating some Asian woman for months, only to be told at the last minute that she couldn't go out with them again because she was getting married next week! I know the "guilty parties" mean well, they don't want to give anyone unpleasant news directly if they don't have to, but I prefer candid discussion to deferential cant.

(Q) Do you agree that Asians have a high degree of hypocrisy? Or is this just a prejudice of the writer?

- **hypocrisy :** showing or expressing feelings, beliefs, or virtues that one does not actually have
- **unsettling :** nervous, confused or upset
- **candid :** direct and open; straightforward
- **deferential :** courteously respectful
- **cant :** insincere, false, or hypocritical statements

PART 2

25 Topical Dialogues

Issue 01 Single Mother's Regimen

F : I remember when we upgraded our computer system. We all thought that our work would get much easier once we learned how to navigate the new system.

M : I gather that that did not happen.

F : Absolutely not! During the transition phase, we had to do everything two times, once the old way that we were used to, and also once the new way. So we worked twice as hard!

M : Any adjustment to novelty is difficult.

F : And, of course, it also took a lot of time and trial-and-error.

M : But, surely, however long, it was just a temporary situation. When you finally mastered the new system, I'm sure everything worked out fine.

F : You mean, other than the continuous upgrades that we undergo?

M : A minor and relatively infrequent happening, I'm sure, and each time the situation improves, doesn't it?

- navigate : deal effectively
- gather : conclude
- transition phase : period between two distinct conditions
- novelty : (sth) new and unusual

F : Of course not! The more technologically advanced our office becomes, the more we are all expected to do. It used to be that if the business grew, new people were hired to handle the overflow. But now the same number of people keep doing more tasks.

M : Why is that so, do you reckon?

F : The way I figure, I used to have X number of things to do every day. Let's say it was X +/- 5, since every day was not exactly the same. But it took about 8 hours to do my job, and then I went home.

M : OK, so then you got a new computer.

F : Right. So I still did my old X +/- 5 tasks, but for a while I did it twice, in the same 8 hours. Although usually I had to work late.

M : So, this was 2 (X +/- 5)?

F : Yes. After a month, it was closer to the old task, though, since we didn't have to duplicate all our work any more. But it never again became X +/-5 in the old way; we never had the luxury of doing our old jobs in less than eight hours, as we thought.

M : What happened?

F : It gradually, though rather quickly, became X + Y + Z. As each task became somewhat simpler because of the computer and other "labor-saving" devices, we simply had more tasks to do. But the number of tasks, and the amount of support and backup work that each task now requires, kept filling all the time available. More than kept pace, in fact. These days, despite all my nifty new tools, I never get to leave the office early. It's usually at least an hour later, and most of the time I end up taking work home with me.

M : Oh?

- **overflow :** excess; too great an amount or quantity
- **reckon :** think or assume
- **luxury :** anything above the level of necessity
- **more than kept pace :** went faster than
- **nifty :** well designed, effective, or easy to use
- **end up :** come to a finish or a final position

F : Yes, that's another big disadvantage. Since the computer in my house is like the one at work, being at home is more and more like being in the office. I feel more and more enslaved, as though I've lost all touch with my private life.

M : It must seem like the job never ends.

F : Exactly!

M : So, what can you do about it?

F : That's a good question! But I don't like the trend of people staying at home to do the work via computer. It's true that they save time traveling back and forth to their job, but they just use that same time doing more work! The problem is not so much the amount of time, it's the erosion of our private lives.

M : Maybe we should have more vacations more often.

F : That might help. But only if we could get some place far away from the phones and faxes and emails! Otherwise, we would just be expanding this erosion on a global basis. We need to be able to "drop out" completely for some very definable period of time, or we're all going to become crazy.

M : You know, this reminds me of sleep.

F : Sleep! Now, there's a novel thought!

M : Sleep is analogous to the modern work situation, I think. The amount of time people spend sleeping is relatively unimportant—the really vital aspect is the quality. Every day or so, people need to have a period of deep sleep. If they don't have that, they become more and more sluggish, and in only a few days they start to lose their sanity.

- **enslave :** make (sb) into a servant
- **trend :** general direction or tendency
- **via :** by means of
- **erode :** lessen or disappear
- **definable :** able to be defined
- **analogous :** similar or parallel in certain ways
- **sluggish :** lacking alertness, vigor, or energy
- **sanity :** soundness of mind

F : I think you captured the situation perfectly. It's not really the time we spend working that is so much the issue, it's our inability to completely and clearly stop working that's the problem.

Questions

1. *Did the man seem sympathetic or indifferent at first? How can you tell?*
2. *Does the woman think the computer is a labor-saving or labor-making invention? Why do you think so?*
3. *In your own words, how is sleep like work?*

→ **capture:** understand, picture, hold

Issue 02 Biggest Lies

M : I don't want to go to work today.

F : I can well imagine! You haven't had a day off in weeks. Why don't you just call in sick?

M : I can't do that. I'm not sick, I just don't feel like going to work today. I'm tired.

F : But you have sick leave accrued. It doesn't do you any good if you don't ever use it.

M : I know. And it doesn't carry over to next year. So if I don't use it, I lose it.

F : I think that's unfair. Your fellow workers take their sick days off and they still get paid for it, but you never do.

M : I just don't think it's right. The purpose of sick leave is to deal with a medical emergency, not just take time off. I get vacation time, you know.

F : But everyone does it! Except you.

M : Just because everyone does it doesn't make it right, you know. That excuse would justify anything, and then where would we be?

F : Where does your honesty get you? You certainly don't get any rewards for it. Nobody hangs a medal on your chest for never telling a lie or bending a rule a little bit.

M : We shouldn't do the right thing just because we expect a reward. We should do it because it's the morally correct thing to do. That's the only way a just society can operate.

F : You call our society morally just? It's full of lying, thieving politicians and crooked businessmen. They just love to take advantage of honest suckers like you.

- **I can well imagine** : I'm not surprised; it is easy to understand (sth)
- **call in sick** : telephone to say (sb) is not coming to work because of illness
- **leave** : permission to be absent, as from work or military duty
- **accrue** : grow or increase over time, especially by adding gradually
- **carry over** : continue to exist
- **where would we be?** : type of rhetorical question (meaning that the answer is self-evident)
- **bend a rule** : do (sth) that is not normally allowed, but will not cause serious problems
- **just** : morally or legally right
- **crooked** : dishonest
- **sucker** : person who is easily taken advantage of

M : But that doesn't mean I have to be like them. If nobody has standards, then there aren't any standards at all.

F : But they're certainly not going to change on your behalf. You might as well get your share of the benefits. Nobody cares.

M : But I care! Just because someone else is a liar doesn't mean that I have to be one too! I may not get much out of this world, but at least I can keep my self-respect. Even if I'm the only one! Isn't that worth something?

F : You can take a load of dignity in one hand and a load of diamonds in the other—which one is going to be worth more?

M : I guess it depends on which scale you measure them on.

Questions

1. *Which person would probably suggest that morality is related to expediency?*
2. *What is the value of a moral code that is not universally applied?*
3. *Why does she call him a sucker? Why doesn't he think he is one?*

- **standards :** the ideas of what is good or normal that (sb) uses to compare one thing with another
- **on (one's) behalf :** for (one's) benefit
- **expediency :** what is useful or necessary to do in a particular situation, even if it is morally wrong

Issue 03 New Year's Vows

F : I give up!
M : Give up what?
F : Every year I make a bunch of resolutions, and I never keep any of them. So I might as well stop.
M : Why do you make them?
F : Because I want to improve my life. But it never does any good. I guess I just don't have enough will power.
M : Maybe the problem is one of "won't power" instead.
F : Huh?
M : Tell me one of your failed resolutions.
F : I said I was going to lose weight. But I've already gained five kilograms!
M : So, all you need to do is fix a very strict regimen and stick to it. How much do you want to lose? There are only two ways to lose weight, eat less or exercise more. (Or a combination of the two.) So, control your intake of calories, every day. Be cruel to yourself. Make yourself walk more, use the stairs instead of the escalator. Pretty soon, your new lifestyle will become a habit, and you won't even have to think about it any more.
F : You make it sound so easy. But it's not, you know. Do you ever make New Year's resolutions?
M : Of course not! There's nothing to change, I'm perfect the way I am!
F : You are not!
M : All right, I'm joking! But I don't make New Year's resolutions. To me, that's just a kind of ritual. People do it every year, but it doesn't mean anything. But I do monitor my failings throughout the year, not just on the 1st of January, and I continuously take steps to improve myself.
F : How well do you do?
M : I guess it depends on what the problem is. Things like dieting and saving more money—those are pretty easy to control, once I make up my mind. I keep a record every day of what I eat and how much I spend, so I

- regimen : a special plan of food, exercise etc. that is intended to improve one's health
- stick to it : keep to a task
- ritual : activity regularly performed in a definite, prescribed, manner

constantly give myself an objective report card. That way I have a way of checking up on how well I'm doing.

F : What about more difficult things, like improving some character fault?

M : You mean you think I have any character faults? I always thought I was Mr. Wonderful!

F : Stop kidding around. I'm serious.

M : OK, I'm sorry. I guess that's one of my imperfections, I make too many jokes.

F : So, what can you do about it?

M : Like you said, this is more difficult. There isn't any quick fix. But, first I have to become aware of the problem, like I am now—thanks to you! So, tonight I'll think about how many times I've done this, and I'll try to do it less often tomorrow. Over time, I think I can do considerably better, even if I never eliminate the defect entirely. But progress is good, even if perfection is out of reach. Right?

F : I don't know whether to admire your self-control or laugh at your naivete.

M : I give you my permission to do both!

Questions

1. *Does the male make sense in his approach to self-improvement, or does he lack sense?*
2. *Who is more serious?*
3. *Why do people fail to keep their resolutions, according to the dialog? (There are at least two answers given.)*

- **serious :** not joking
- **quick fix :** fast solution to some problem, often on a temporary basis
- **eliminate :** get rid of; remove
- **naivete :** state of being innocently naive, ignorant, immature, unrealistic, idealistic

Issue 04 Friends with Stress

F : Stress can be momentum for a successful life.

M : Really? How so?

F : In the same way that necessity is the mother of invention: it is a constant prod to accomplishment.

M : You mean that you think if people are left to their own devices, they won't get much done on their own?

F : Sure. It's just like societies. People who live in pleasant weather conditions where food is plentiful, so they never have to work very hard to survive, usually don't amount to much. Their natural indolence is not punished in any Darwinian or environmental sense. But the groups who have to struggle constantly are the ones who generally accomplish the most. They have to work hard just to exist, and the diligence itself pays high dividends.

M : How does that relate to stress?

F : Well, nobody wants stress. We would all prefer to take a nice nap when we're tired, or take a day off now and then to relax. But if we're under a lot of pressure to produce some result, we'll ignore our natural laziness in order to get it done.

- **momentum :** the ability to keep increasing, developing, or being more successful
- **prod :** stimulus to action
- **amount to much :** accomplish important things or achieve high personal value
- **indolence :** laziness
- **dividend :** benefit or advantage

M : Won't the expectation of success do the same thing?

F : Are you asking if virtue is its own reward?

M : No. That only works with a few individuals. But don't people work hard to get ahead?

F : There are two principles that guide human behavior: hope and fear. One works better than the other for different people, but most folks respond more strongly to just one of them, fear. Fear of being fired or losing status will motivate more people than the desire for self-promotion. Nevertheless, both principles entail stress; the difference is that in one case the stress is generated externally and in the other internally.

Questions

1. *What is the difference between working out of the expectation of reward and believing that virtue is its own reward?*
2. *What are the most motivating factors, according to the passage?*
3. *How is the stress produced by each of those two factors different?*

- **fired** : dismissed
- **entail** : cause or involve by necessity or as a consequence

Issue 05 Money Doesn't Guarantee Happiness

M : How does anyone achieve happiness?

F : It depends on what you mean by happiness, I guess.

M : To me, happiness is having the physical means to lead a rich, varied life.

F : That means health and wealth, then, right?

M : More or less. No one can be "too healthy," of course, but maybe it's possible to be too rich.

F : How?

M : If money becomes more important than anything else. Money is a tool to use for creating the good life, but it is not an end unto itself.

F : What are the other tools?

M : A healthy body—though I suppose we don't have much control over that, other than taking care of what we have.

F : And?

M : A good mind: maintaining an open attitude towards life, staying curious about the world. Actively reading and thinking about the human condition.

F : Religion?

M : Maybe. But I think serious nonreligious people can achieve the same kinds of happiness as believers. Religion is often a great thing for the individual, but overly religious societies are usually too narrow to promote much happiness.

F : What about democracy?

---

other than : (sth) else; besides

M : Any government will get in the way of a person's absolute happiness, if complete freedom is a component of that. But it's all relative. I suppose private happiness is attainable even in the harshest totalitarian society, and for some people utterly unreachable even in the most utopian.

F : You know, I've been reading about the old Cynics.

M : Yeah? You mean the Greek philosophers?

F : Sure. Like Diogenes.

M : The guy with the lamp, looking for an honest man?

F : Right. They thought that happiness is attained by ridding oneself of necessities, not by acquiring wealth. The fewer things we need, the happier we are.

M : Okay.

F : For instance—I think it was Diogenes—one of them saw a young boy at the well drinking water from his cupped hands. The Cynic extolled how much wisdom we can learn from children, and threw away his own drinking cup as being unnecessary.

M : Hmmm. I don't think most people would agree with that notion.

F : Maybe that's why so few are happy.

Questions

1. *What goes into happiness?*
2. *Is it possible for anyone to have too much health? Explain your answer.*
3. *What lesson did the child teach the Cynic?*

- **in the way :** in a position that blocks or interferes
- **totalitarian :** relating to a centralized government that does not allow differing opinion
- **rid :** free or relieve of (sth) unwanted
- **extol :** praise highly

Issue 06 Household Chores

F : I'm tired of doing all the work around here! Let's share some of the chores around the house.

M : But when I get home from work, it's late and I'm tired. I just want to relax and go to bed.

F : But I work too, you know. But I end up being stuck with two jobs, one at home and one at the office.

M : What can I do about it?

F : You can start coming home a lot earlier and helping me.

M : But I make more money than you do. So my job is more important.

F : What difference does that make? If we weren't a two-income family, what would we have? Do you just want me to quit and look after the house by myself?

M : No, of course not. And it's not just the money; we could get by on my salary. But I know you get a lot of satisfaction out of your profession. I wouldn't want to deprive you of that.

F : Then you'll help me?

M : Insofar as I can. What do you want me to do?

F : Why don't you cook three evenings a week, and I'll wash the dishes those nights? The other days, we'll switch tasks.

M : OK, that sounds reasonable enough. I bet you didn't know I'm a pretty good cook!

F : I've heard you tell me that hundreds of times, but I've never seen you demonstrate!

M : All right. I'll start tomorrow. What else?

F : There's lots to be done. Cleaning the bathroom,

→ end up : reach a final state or condition
→ get by : manage to live

washing the clothes, ironing, shopping, sweeping the floors, putting things away. Sometimes it seems endless.

M : OK, I'll tell you what. Make a list of chores that have to be done every single day and those that have to be done less often, once a week or whatever, and I'll draw up a schedule. We can talk about how to divide up the jobs so that it's even.

F : And then there are the ongoing projects. Washing the windows, putting up new wallpaper, that sort of thing. There's no schedule, really, but they all have to be done sooner or later.

M : Then write each of these down on a separate piece of paper, and I'll do the same thing. We'll put them all in a jar. When either one of us has some spare time, we'll draw one of the pieces of paper and do it!

F : That's a good idea. But we need to commit to spending at least two or three hours every week on these things.

M : It's a deal. But, of course, there are some weeks when I just can't commit myself. You know how my job is.

F : If you can't, you can't! But then you should pay some kind of penalty. For every week that you don't spend on these chores, you have to both cook and clean dishes the same night.

M : Agreed. As long, of course, as you make the same commitment.

F : OK. Let's shake on it!

Questions

1. *What are they going to do about everyday chores?*
2. *What have they agreed to do about the irregular jobs around the house?*
3. *How would you solve a similar problem? Can you think of any other solutions?*

- **draw up :** write, compose
- **even :** of equal worth
- **deal :** agreement
- **shake on it :** shake hands to seal an agreement

Issue 07 The Perfect Woman and How to Make Her

M : How are you? You look great!

F : Thanks for saying so. But I'm always tired. I have a cold that I just can't seem to shake.

M : Have you seen a doctor?

F : Sure, but it doesn't help.

M : I think you should gain a little weight back. Maybe you're just too thin.

F : No, I don't think so. It took me a long time to discipline myself against overeating. I don't want to break all my good habits.

M : Your drive is admirable, but don't you think you've taken it a bit too far? When I saw you before, I didn't think you were too heavy—you always looked very good—but you were always so full of energy back then. Everyone needs some fat on his body to store energy and resist disease.

F : No, I think you're wrong. In fact, I plan on losing more. I want to be able to wear a new dress I saw, but I'm still a little big for it.

M : You mean you're sacrificing your vitality for the sake of your vanity?

F : Look, I've thought about this a lot. Women may have become more equal to men than they were a few decades ago, but it's still a male-dominated world. Women who look good to men do better and go further than the ones who don't. And I'm determined to go as far as I can in life. If that means losing some weight and keeping it off, that's a small sacrifice to make. And besides, I think being thin is probably healthier than being fat, anyway.

M : We're not talking about being obese—that is a very

- shake : remove (sth)
- discipline : train by instruction and practice
- drive : energy, ambition
- sacrifice : give (sth) up for (sth else) considered to be of greater value
- vanity : excessive pride; conceit
- dominate : rule over by superior power or authority
- obese : extremely fat

dangerous condition and needs to be dealt with. But we are talking about being fat enough to meet our basic metabolic needs. Artificially skinny people just don't stand up well to microbes and fatigue; whatever gains you make now are short-lived, and will end up costing you too much in the future. You're already complaining about being tired!

F : I know what I'm doing. Basically, I feel fine. I just need to lose a little bit more and then stabilize my weight, and everything will be back to normal again.

Questions

1. *What is the value of weight?*
2. *Why would anyone want to be thin?*
3. *What do you think a feminist would say about the woman's attitude?*

- **skinny :** very thin
- **stand up to :** withstand
- **microbe :** microorganism, especially a bacterium, that causes disease
- **stabilize :** make (sth) stable
- **feminist :** (sb) who supports equal rights and opportunities for women

Issue 08 Know Yourself

M : There's a personality quiz in this magazine. Do you want to take it together?

F : Why not? Where is it?

M : I'm looking for it now. Here it is!

F : OK. Let's get started. What's the first question?

M : "If you had an afternoon to yourself, would you rather read a book on philosophy or take a walk on the beach?"

F : Well, obviously, I'd rather read. People shouldn't waste time being idle if they can improve their mind.

M : Really? I always pictured you as more the outdoors type.

F : Just goes to show you how much you know!

M : OK. Number 2: "Have you ever traveled to another country?"

F : Why, many times, of course!

M : I never knew that. Where did you go?

F : Is that the next question?

M : No, I was just curious.

F : Then let's go on. We can chit-chat later.

M : All right, then. "In the course of a year, do you spend more money on make-up/health-care products or books?"

chit-chat : talk easily or casually

F : You should know that! The right answer is books!

M : What about all that money you spent on cosmetics last week?

F : That was last week! It said "over the course of a year," didn't it?

M : Yes, it sure did.

F : Well, over an entire year I spend lots more money on books than on frivolous things like make-up!

M : But I never see you reading anything!

F : Do you have me under surveillance or something?

M : No, of course not.

F : Then, you don't know how I spend all my time, do you? Let's go on to the next question.

M : "Do you feel that you are an honest person?"

F : Absolutely! Why would anyone ever say No to that?

M : When you take these personality quizzes, do you try to answer the way you really feel or the way you think you should?

F : It's like any other game. High score wins, right?

M : There isn't any score, it's just a way of trying to find out who you really are.

F : I know who I am! But it's also important to know what you should be, don't you think?

Questions

1. *How many questions do you think the woman answered honestly? Why do you think so?*
2. *What is her attitude toward taking personality quizzes?*
3. *Try to describe her personality with at least five adjectives.*

→ frivolous : not deserving of serious attention

→ surveillance : close observation of a person or group, esp. by a law-enforcement or intelligence-gathering agency

Issue 09

TV Channel

M : Hey! I was watching that!

F : You didn't seem to be watching it. It didn't look like you were paying much attention to it at all. So I changed the channel to see something better, that's all.

M : But you interrupted my football game!

F : It's the same game every time. Only the names and the uniforms change every week, that's all. So, this time we're going to watch something we can both enjoy together.

M : Certainly not this show! It's just a stupid drama. These aren't real people, you know, they're just actors. It's all pretense. At least the game I was watching is genuine!

F : We have all these men running into each other all the time, trying to score points with a silly little ball. You call that genuine? After all, what difference does it actually make who wins or what the score is?

M : It matters to me!

F : But why? What do you get out of it? Does it pay your bills or make you any better looking or more intelligent than you already are?

M : Watching it makes me feel better, more relaxed. I enjoy watching football, the same way you like your soap operas. Do they make you any richer or better? No, of course not!

F : But at least they engage my attention throughout. You usually sleep through most of your games.

M : Look, I'm tired and just want to relax. Even if my eyes are closed, I can still hear the game, you know. And if something exciting happens, I pay closer attention then.

F : Why don't we watch something together? We don't spend enough time in each other's company any more. We just don't communicate enough.

- **interrupt :** stop the action of (sb) or (sth)
- **pretense :** false appearance
- **genuine :** not false; real or pure
- **matter :** be important; have a big effect on what happens
- **soap opera :** television or radio series about the imaginary lives of a group people

M : You might be right. That sounds like a good idea. Why don't we go back to the game, and I can tell you what's going on?

F : That's not what I had in mind. I understand the game of football; I don't need you to explain it to me—I just find it all very boring, that's all.

M : Okay, then, why don't we find a music channel, or some variety show? That way we can both appreciate the same thing at the same time. Will that make you happy?

F : Oh! Very happy! You can even choose which one we'll see—I like them all, especially one I can share with you.

M : All right, then, let me have the remote control. While we're making our selection, do you mind if I just check the score, real quick?

F : You're incorrigible.[*]

Questions

1. Why doesn't she like football?

2. Why doesn't he like TV dramas?

3. Can you suggest some activity (other than watching television) that might make them both happy?

---

incorrigible : impossible to reform; not easily changed

Issue 10 Dad Hates My Boyfriend

M : I'm worried about my son's girl friend.

F : Why? Is she sick?

M : Not as far as I know. But I just don't think she's suitable for him.

F : Why not? What's wrong with her?

M : It's hard to put my finger on, exactly. In many ways, she seems like a wonderful person.

F : Then what's the problem?

M : I don't think she'll make him happy in the long run.

F : Why not?

M : She just seems flighty. Like she can't stick with anything for the long haul. She needs too much attention all the time.

F : It seems to me that you should be worried more about her than your son.

M : Why do you say that?

F : Well, all you seem concerned about is whether she's "suitable" for him, that she won't "make him happy." That "she needs too much attention." It all seems one-sided, that her only role is to take care of his needs and that he doesn't have any reciprocal responsibility towards her.

M : That's not what I meant! But, naturally, I'm more concerned about my son's well-being than hers. She's just a stranger, but he's my own flesh and blood.

F : You know, she might be your daughter soon. Then what?

M : I hope not! I'll do everything I can to keep that from happening!

F : Leave them alone to make up their own minds. It's their future, not yours, you know.

M : But what do they know? They're too young to make a decision like this on their own. Especially my son. He's not in his right mind. She's already got him under her spell.

F : Maybe they have each other under a spell. Sounds like love to me.

M : Love! What does that have to do with anything? Love

- put (one's) finger on : be able to identify precisely
- flighty : changing opinions and behavior often; not serious or reliable
- long haul : long period of time
- reciprocal : mutual
- spell : magical charm; strong influence

doesn't pay the bills or take care of the problems of being married.

F : No, it doesn't. But it helps put those bills and problems in perspective. And it helps justify why they need to be dealt with.

M : Whose side are you on, anyway?

F : I'm on theirs! None of us can see the future. Sometimes love isn't enough. And sometimes love itself is not real or permanent. Bad things happen. We all make some bad choices in life. But we can't know in advance how things may turn out, either. Sometimes we have to take a chance and hope we do the right thing.

M : That's why I won't stand for them to get married. I know it's wrong!

F : You don't know, you just think so. You might even be right. But sometimes we just have to butt out and let our children take care of their own affairs of the heart. They know their own needs and desires much more than we do; they have to live with them every day, but we're outsiders in that regard. We're just observers, even if we want to be more than that.

M : I can't just let my son throw his life away!

F : Then talk to him. Let him know how you feel. Tell him why you think he should find a different potential wife. Do the best you can to convince him that it's a bad choice. But you have to let him decide on his own, or you'll both regret it.

Questions

1. *What's wrong with the son's girlfriend?*
2. *Should parents have a veto over who their children's spouse will be?*
3. *What is her advice?*

- **put (sth) in perspective :** place a problem in a proper relationship
- **stand for :** tolerate; allow
- **butt out :** stop interfering in (sth) that does not concern (sb)
- **affairs of the heart :** matters connected with love
- **throw (one's) life away :** ruin (one's) life or potential
- **observer :** inactive watcher
- **veto :** clear refusal to give permission of any sort

Issue 11 *Thanksgiving Every Day*

F : How can you be so chipper all the time?

M : I just don't let things bring me down, that's all. I figured out a long time ago that the world would never be perfect, but I was bound to make the best of it that I could. So I try not to let bad situations get me down.

F : You do an admirable job of it! You never look depressed.

M : You'd be surprised. Sometimes I feel utterly defeated, when nothing is going my way. But I don't ever try to show it. I try not to let on how hopeless the situation is, I just bear down and shoulder the problem as well as I can. And eventually things get better again.

F : Most people I know just develop a chip on their shoulder when things don't go well. They become surly and

- chipper : happy
- bring (one) down : cause (sb) or (sth) to fall or lose power
- figure out : think about a problem or situation until it is solved
- bound : determined
- let on : admit
- bear down : work hard, make a special effort
- shoulder : accept a difficult or unpleasant responsibility, duty, etc.
- have a chip on (one's) shoulder : be constantly angry or ready to quarrel or fight
- surly : bad-tempered, unfriendly, rude

blame everybody else for their problems. Or they just give up.

M : That's one way of coping with the situation, I guess. For some people, it's effective; it's all a matter of personality. It lets them get on with life until things get better. But it sure takes its toll on family and friendship, and it doesn't accomplish very much. I'd rather smile my way through life than frown. Eventually, at the end, I'll get to the same place, but I'll have a more pleasant itinerary, I think.

F : I wish I had more of your optimism.

M : It's all a matter of constant training, actually. Every situation is potentially good and bad. Just try to concentrate on the good as much as you can, and it gets easier as time goes by.

Questions

1. *How can one develop a positive view of life?*
2. *How much good is it to be resentful or defeatist?*
3. *Describe the "travel through life" metaphor used in the dialogue.*

- get on : continue, proceed, or progress
- take its toll : have a very bad effect
- frown : make an angry, unhappy, or confused expression, moving (one's) eyebrows together
- itinerary : trip
- potentially : possibly
- resentful : feeling angry and unhappy
- defeatist : believing that (one) will not succeed
- metaphor : way of describing (sth) by comparing it to (sth) else

Issue 12 Lower Your Expectations

M : I never feel like I'm good enough.

F : What are you talking about? You have an important position not only in your company but in fact in the entire country, you have far more money than most people even dream of, and you're still young and vigorous. What else could anyone want?

M : I don't know. But whatever I've done isn't enough as far as my father is concerned.

F : I'm sure he's very proud of you.

M : I doubt that. He sure doesn't act like it!

F : You must be exaggerating.

M : I don't think so.

F : Why not?

M : Well, he always spent a lot of money and time on me. I always had private tutors and expert advisers to help me. But, when I got accepted to the best university in the country, he never even said congratulations. He just reminded me of all he had done to make it possible, without even giving me any credit for my accomplishment at all.

F : I guess he just has trouble expressing himself. A lot of men are like that, I guess.

M : He doesn't have any trouble expressing his disapproval! I was number two in my class, and he berated me for being second best! Then I went to grad school and graduated number one, and he told me that I wasn't competing against other people, only against myself—and I should have done better!

F : My! He does sound hard.

M : Hard isn't the word! Every step of the way, he's been behind me pushing, pushing, pushing. When I fell down, he never gave me a hand, he just stood there telling me to get up and get going! But no matter where

- **credit :** approval or praise for some act or quality
- **berate :** scold (sb) severely
- **grad :** graduate

I have gotten, he's never had a kind word for me, just a negative comparison to someone else who had done it younger or with a higher score or with more grace.

F : But did he ever abandon you when you failed? Did he ever comfort you and let you become self-satisfied?

M : No, of course not. If I ever stayed a failure, he wouldn't be able to brag about my achievements to his friends!

F : He does that? You've heard him?

M : Many times, when he thought I wouldn't hear. Around them, you'd think I was the greatest thing in his life!

F : You probably are. He obviously loves you and is very proud of you.

M : I don't doubt that at all. But I wish he'd show me sometime, not just his buddies!

Questions

1. What is the man's complaint about his father?

2. Who is more responsible for the son's success, himself or his father?

3. Do you think this father loves his son? Explain your answer.

Issue 13 Positively Negative

F : Hey, I just found a great word! The same word covers the entire spectrum of its domain.

M : What do you mean?

F : That's the word!

M : What's the word?

F : Mean.

M : Mean? How do you mean?

F : No, that's a different sense of mean. It's not the one I mean.

M : I think I'm lost. What are you talking about?

F : Mean!

M : Don't be mean! Let me in on your joke.

F : That's another meaning of mean, but it's outside the scope of what I was talking about.

M : OK, I give up. Will you please explain to me what the word is and what "domain spectrum" you're referring to?

F : The word is "mean".

M : So are you. But please continue.

F : The domain is "quality." Mean can mean anything along that entire range of meaning.

- **mean** : cruel
- **let (sb) in on (sth)** : inform (sb) about (sth)
- **domain spectrum** : range within a field
- **refer to** : mention (sb) or (sth)

M : How is that possible?

F : Well, if I made you a sandwich ...

M : Would you do that? I'm suddenly very hungry!

F : Maybe a little later, don't interrupt me. If I made you one, you might say, "Wow! You make a mean sandwich!" Right? What would you mean by that? Especially if you were an American?

M : It's the same thing as saying that it was a great sandwich.

F : Yes, of course. But if you were a Brit, you'd probably use "mean" in the sense of "ungenerous" or "skimpy." Right?

M : I guess so. So the same word is at both ends of the spectrum! That's neat!

F : But it doesn't stop there! "Mean" is also just the technical word for "average," so it's not only used at both ends but in the middle too!

M : Wow! You're right! So, why don't you make me a mean sandwich, now?

F : OK. But, in what sense of "mean"? Do you want an average one?

M : In the great sense, of course!

Questions

1. *How many meanings of the word "mean" can you find in the dialogue?*
2. *To pun is to use language in a playful way, based on sound or appearance rather than meaning. Can you find any examples of punning?*
3. *In a conversation, how would one know which sense of "mean" would be meant?*

- **skimpy :** not large enough in amount or size
- **neat :** interesting

Issue 14 Pet People and Their Trouble

F : Look at that silly person! He has to get up this early, bundle up to keep warm, and go outside every day just to walk his dog!

M : Yeah. And then he has to do the same thing again tonight.

F : He probably has to do this several times a day!

M : And even then, there's the inevitable mess occasionally. But, even if the dog is perfectly housebroken, the place still smells like a dog. And there's hair everywhere. Nobody wants to visit such a home.

F : And he carries the dog around with him whenever he goes shopping. He puts that goofy little sweater on the dog, and away they go! The dog doesn't even have to walk.

M : Actually, I feel sort of embarrassed for the dog's sake. No self-respecting dog would make himself look so ridiculous!

F : Well, I suppose that is better than having most of its fur cut off, having its ears dyed, or getting its tail bobbed.

- **bundle up :** dress warmly or snugly
- **walk the dog :** take a dog outside so that it can walk, run, play
- **housebreak :** train a pet to excrete outdoors or in a specific place
- **goofy :** foolish; silly; ridiculous
- **self-respecting :** having regard for oneself
- **bob :** cut short

M : You're right about that!

F : And he talks to, and about, the dog, just as though it's a human being.

M : Dogs are dogs, not people. They are pets, not family members. Why can't they be treated that way?

F : People must be extremely lonely or socially maladjusted if they have to make friends with four-legged creatures.

M : Maybe it's the illusion of affection. Dogs never criticize anybody's actions, they bark and wag their tails when their owners come home, they lick their faces and show off for attention.

F : And if they are ignored, they don't file for divorce or leave home.

M : They certainly know where their meal ticket is!

F : A certain respect and appreciation for nonhuman life forms is a good trait. We should all work to prevent cruel, inhumane treatment of animals.

M : But that doesn't mean we should treat animals better than we treat other people.

F : I wonder what he thinks about eating dog? Do you suppose he thinks it's okay, as long as we don't devour pets?

M : That's a good question! But I bet he hasn't really thought about it.

F : Maybe vegetarianism is a good idea—perhaps we should stop killing animals for food. That seems pretty inhumane!

M : It would never work. Humans are, biologically, carnivorous. We need to eat meat.

- **maladjusted** : badly or poorly fitted to (one's) social circumstances
- **illusion** : mistaken idea or belief
- **meal ticket** : basic support
- **trait** : distinctive feature, as of a person's character
- **inhumane** : lacking pity or compassion
- **devour** : eat (sth) greedily and completely
- **vegetarianism** : eating only plants
- **carnivorous** : meat-eating

F : No, we don't have to. Actually, we're not carnivorous—we're omnivorous. We can get all the nutrients we need from nonmeat sources.

M : And I suppose you're against hunting, too?

F : Of course, I am! Talk about cruel!

M : It's no more cruel than raising animals for their eventual slaughter.

F : But those animals were never wild. It's always been their destiny to be butchered. And modern methods of dispatching them are very humane, so the beasts don't needlessly suffer. It's not like hunting them down and then ruthlessly exterminating them.

M : Most animals need to be culled, or they'll overrun their ecological niche. And then they'll face massive starvation. A swift killing is much better than slowly dying of hunger.

F : That's what they said about all those species of animals that have been hunted to extinction!

M : Most countries do a pretty good job of limiting hunting to strict quotas at only certain times of the year. More effort needs to be made, on the issue of mass commercial fishing in particular, but effective management of wildlife is possible, I think. At least, hunting and fishing are conducted to keep people from starving. It's not like trapping and beating animals to death just so their hides can be stripped off and made into fur coats for rich old women.

- omnivorous : eating all kinds of food
- talk about : expression indicating strong agreement
- slaughter : the killing of animals for food
- butcher : slaughter or prepare animals for market
- dispatch : put (sb) or (sth) to death quickly
- exterminate : destroy a species or group completely
- cull : remove unwanted members
- niche : situation or activity specially suited to a certain character
- quota : assigned limit or amount
- hide : animal skin

F : Now, wait a minute! These furs not only look great, but they keep us warm. We'd freeze without them.

M : Maybe at the Poles, but most places are not cold enough to need them. And even there, modern synthetic materials are much more effective at retaining heat. The only excuse for the fur industry is human vanity!

F : Not any more vanity is involved than for some "brave hunter" to slaughter some defenseless beast with a high-powered automatic rifle—maybe from the air!—just so he can hang a stuffed head on the wall!

Questions

1. What is the pet lover criticized for? Give as many answers as you can.

2. Summarize the two attitudes about hunting.

3. Discuss the pros and cons of wearing furs.

vanity : excessive pride; conceit

Issue 15 Can You Please Put Out Your Cigarette?

F : Would you mind not smoking, please?

M : Sure. Sorry.

F : Thank you.

M : You're welcome. Actually, I take that back.[+] You're not welcome at all!

F : What?

M : You heard me. I'm pretty tired of people like you interfering with my rights. This is a public place, it's perfectly legal to smoke here, and I'm minding my own business. Please bother someone else and leave me alone.

F : I beg your pardon! This is indeed a public place, and I have rights here, too! You are not minding your own

[+] take (sth) back : rescind (sth)

business if you are smoking, you're bothering me and everyone else who doesn't like the smell of smoke.

M : I don't like the smell of your perfume, but I don't try to keep you from wearing it.

F : I'm sorry if the odor of my perfume offends you, but it doesn't hurt you any. Your smoke irritates my lungs and makes me sick.

M : And I am allergic to perfumes. See how my skin is turning red? All because of you!

F : I'm really sorry about that. But it's only a very small number of people, like you, who are bothered by my perfume. Your cigarette smoke endangers everyone.

M : So does all the smog in the air. So do the chemicals in the water we drink. So do the cars that drive by—get hit by any one of them! But you still breathe, drink, and drive, don't you?

F : It's not the same thing. Second-hand smoke has been proven to be even more dangerous to non-smokers than to the ones who smoke!

M : Then, lady, my advice to you is to start smoking. You'll be better off that way!

F : You certainly are rude!

M : Listen. I've been smoking most of my life. I'm not a heavy smoker at all, I know the health hazards involved. But I enjoy a nice cigarette after a big meal. It makes digestion better and creates a very mellow mood before I have to

- **odor :** smell; scent (esp. in a negative sense)
- **better off :** in an improved condition
- **hazard :** danger
- **mellow :** free from tension; pleasantly agreeable

go back to work. I make sure that I'm either with other smokers or far away from non-smokers.

F : Not far enough.

M : To be "far enough" I'd have to be on a different planet, as far as you are concerned. But I know I was so far away that you couldn't smell my smoke. You really don't have anything to complain about.

F : I can smell your cigarette from much farther away than that. Just because the smoke dissipates in the air doesn't mean that the smell and the chemicals don't travel pretty far. If you weren't bothering me, I wouldn't have said anything to you.

M : Even the sight of someone smoking bothers you! You just can't stand for someone to find a little pleasure in this world.

F : Don't be ridiculous. There are many pleasurable activities that don't include smoking. As a matter of fact, I think smoking distracts from everything and makes even very enjoyable activities a lot less fun.

M : That's you! But a lot of other people enjoy a good cigarette now and then. I don't tell you how to have a good time; don't try to enforce your rules on me.

F : I have rights, too!

M : But so do I! I'm getting sick and tired of being treated like a second-class citizen just because I smoke. I'm sick of having to go outside in the cold just to take a break at

---

- **dissipate :** become scattered in various directions
- **stand for :** put up with; tolerate
- **distract :** draw away or divert; prevent concentration

work and enjoy a little stimulation. I'm tired of people like you interfering with my own personal behavior and treating me like a criminal. If you don't want to smoke yourself, that's fine. Just stop trying to keep me from smoking, that's all!

Questions

1. *From her perspective, list the reasons why he should stop smoking there.*
2. *From his perspective, list the reasons why his smoking is not any of her business.*
3. *Why does he resent her interference?*

- **perspective :** point of view
- **resent :** feel offended by

Issue 16 Working Mom vs Non-Working Mom

M : You look beat!

F : I am! Holding down a full-time job and taking care of my kids at the same time is tough work.

M : Why don't you quit your job?

F : What do you mean?

M : Well, you can't give up your children. So why don't you stop working instead?

F : Tired as I am, I've never really seriously considered doing that.

M : Why not?

F : Well, for one thing, our family needs the money. Lots of unexpected expenses have plagued us lately, really eating into our savings. We even had to borrow some money from relatives!

M : I can understand the pressure to work now, then, but the crisis will pass, you know. Why don't you quit when things return to normal?

F : Aside from the money, I don't want to be cooped up indoors all day doing nothing. I enjoy my work. I like the people I deal with, and it is never boring.

M : But what about your children? Shouldn't you spend more time with them?

F : Now that they are all in school, probably not. They leave early in the morning, the same time I do. And I get back just a little later than they do. The only real problem is if somebody's sick. Then I usually have to call in and report that I'll be absent. Fortunately, this seldom happens.

- **beat :** exhausted; worn-out
- **hold down :** have and keep
- **plague :** annoy or bother (sb)
- **eat into :** use up; consume gradually or slowly
- **cooped up :** kept inside or in a small space

M : But don't you just take your work home with you? Even when you're with your children at night, do you really spend any quality time with them?

F : I hardly ever have anything to do after I leave the office. Once in a while, maybe, but I do it after the kids are in bed.

M : But then you just have an even longer day, and you get even more tired.

F : Sure. Once in a while. But it's not a regular occurrence.

M : What would you do if you had to finish your work at home on most days? Would you quit then?

F : I don't know. I've never thought about it. If that happened, and it was a temporary situation, I don't think it would make any difference. If it were permanent, or long-term, I might consider quitting. But even then, I'd just look for another job somewhere else.

M : So you have no intention to stop working?

F : No. Absolutely not. I don't know what I'd do with myself if I didn't have some kind of job to go to every day. It's addicting!

M : That's what smokers and alcoholics say, too.

F : Maybe I'm a workaholic. But I like to keep busy.

Questions

1. *Why doesn't she stop working? Give several answers.*
2. *How has her life changed recently? How might it change?*
3. *In what way is working like a drug dependency?*

workaholic : (sb) with a compulsive need to work all the time

Issue 17 A Marriage Between the Haves and Have-nots

M : It seems like whenever I zig, my wife zags.

F : I know the feeling. Sometimes it is as though my husband and I belong to different species.

M : How can two people stay separated by the same language? Whatever I say seems to mean something else to her.

F : Was it always this way?

M : Maybe. But it seems to me that my wife and I used to understand each other, even if we didn't always agree.

F : I feel the same way. But, gradually, we drifted apart. Our lives became very different, and we lost much of our common ground.

M : I don't think it has anything to do with intention. I still love my wife as much as I ever did, and I think she feels the same about me. But we live separate lives, nevertheless. We just don't communicate very well anymore.

F : In my case, we communicate, but the message is always mixed. We hardly ever agree any more, and even when we do it is with ill grace. Unlike you, I can't say that we still love each other. We've been very unhappy together.

M : I see other couples who have been together for decades, and they still seem to have a very vibrant relationship. They act like they're still teenagers in love. And I wonder how they manage to stay that way for so long.

F : They're very lucky, I guess.

M : Do you think they have some secret that we could learn?

F : They must have one. But I don't know if we could learn anything from them. I think I did my best, I don't think I could do any better than I did, but it just didn't work.

M : It seldom does. Husbands and wives both invest too much of their psyche into their relationship, and each

- **whenever (sb) zigs, (sb else) zags :** when (sb) moves in one direction, (sb else) moves in a different direction
- **drift apart :** slowly move off
- **with ill grace :** grudgingly, with reluctance
- **vibrant :** lively and exciting
- **psyche :** human soul, spirit, mind, or being

one wants too much from it. They both end up frustrated and disappointed that they don't get everything they want. But it's impossible entirely to give up all of one's own ego.

F : My experience is just the opposite. I don't think people give enough of themselves to their lover. They are too selfish and indifferent, and want more out of the relationship than they're willing to give. That's what the real problem is!

Questions

1. *In what way are the two marriages similar?*
2. *How are they different?*
3. *Analyze why each one thinks marriages fail.*

Issue 18 *Panhandling*

M : Look at that poor woman!

F : Which one?

M : That beggar over there. Doesn't she look pathetic?

F : She certainly does. But don't give her anything!

M : Why not? I couldn't live with myself if I didn't help her. For me, it's just spare change. For her, it might mean the difference between eating and starving.

F : I admit that's a possibility, but I'd say the odds against it are astronomically high.

M : Why do you say that?

F : She probably makes more than you do!

M : I doubt that!

F : Just figure it out for yourself. If everybody gives her something every three minutes, and she works only an eight-hour day, how much do you think she takes in? And it's all tax-free!

M : But if that's the case, why would she humiliate herself this way if she didn't need the money?

F: Because she makes more this way than she could by working, of course!

M : I still think I have to help her. What if she really is starving? I couldn't bear to be apathetic in the face of someone's misfortune if there were some way I could help.

F : That's very noble of you. But it's also very gullible. That's exactly the kind of attitude that she rides right to the bank.

- **pathetic :** causing sympathy or sorrow
- **change :** coins
- **odds :** probability
- **astronomical :** too large to be easily imagined; immense
- **humiliate :** lower the pride or self-respect of (sb)
- **apathetic :** feeling or showing little or no interest; indifferent
- **gullible :** easily deceived or tricked
- **ride right to the bank :** exploit for (one's) personal gain

M : How do you know so much?

F : When I was a kid, I used to "spare-change" people all the time. At first, it was just an adventure. I didn't really need the money, but I was in school and didn't have the time for a real job. And then I found out how much I could make doing it just in my spare time. Every week, the amount I took home was truly phenomenal—and I was only panhandling part-time! Think how much the pros must make!

M : Well, all of this is news to me. I've never thought about any of this.

F : I had a friend who needed a lot of money. He knew how much these guys make, so he went into "business" hustling the hustlers. He actually went to the panhandlers with a sob story and wheedled money from them! In just six months, he worked himself completely out of debt.

M : What did he do then? Stay in the business?

F : No. He used his experience to go into politics. Today he's the mayor of a big city. The skills are the same, he says, but now he doesn't have to work outdoors in bad weather.

Questions

1. *Why does the woman oppose helping needy people?*
2. *Why does the man insist it's the right thing to do?*
3. *What skills do you think politicians and panhandlers have in common?*

- **spare-change :** beg for small amounts of unnecessary money
- **phenomenal :** extremely impressive or surprising
- **hustling the hustlers :** getting money from the con men
- **wheedle :** persuasively beg for (sth)
- **in common :** of a shared aspect

Issue 19 Platonic Friends

F : You remember all that talk we had about platonic relationships?

M : Sure. I think it's possible to have close friendships with people of the opposite sex, and you don't.

F : No, I know better. Men are only after one thing from women, and that's sex!

M : I don't want to argue with you about this, but I know you're wrong. Men and women are equally human and have many things other than sex to bring into their relationships.

F : I don't want to argue, either.

M : Then why did you bring the subject up?

F : I just found out something!

M : Yes? What?

F : Well, "platonic friendships" doesn't really mean nonsexual relationships between men and women.

M : What does it mean, then? I always hear it used in that sense.

F : Yes, of course, we commonly use it that way. But it isn't what the expression really means!

M : OK, then, please. Tell me what it actually means.

F : It refers to Plato's love for a much younger man. It's all about homosexual relationships!

M : Really? But Plato was a great philosopher. He always seems so intellectual and unfeeling. I can't imagine his being gay.

F : Homosexuality was not uncommon among the ancient Greeks. They wrote about it constantly, in the most romantic kinds of ways. They wrote lots of poems celebrating same-sex fantasies and experiences. Even the great heroes, like Achilles and Alexander the Great, had male lovers.

M : This is all news to me. It's hard to believe.

F : But it's true. And Sappho of Lesbos was a famous woman poet who wrote about her desires for other women. That's where "Lesbian" gets its meaning.

- **after :** in pursuit of
- **homosexual :** having sexual feelings for members of the same sex
- **unfeeling :** not sympathetic; hard-hearted
- **gay :** homosexual
- **lesbian :** homosexual woman

M : Wait a minute! I've read a lot of Greek poetry. I've never noticed this phenomenon.

F : Oh, the Greeks wrote a lot of heterosexual verse, too, of course. And I suppose most of the translators have deliberately softened the homosexual nature of the rest, making it less obvious and, so, more palatable to most modern readers.

M : But, even so! Plato? I always think of his "Republic" and "Critias." I can't really see him as a very romantic fellow, with either sex.

F : Shows you how much you know! He was also a major poet.

M : Really? You mean philosophical poetry?

F : No, mainly love poems. About men.

M : I'm dumbfounded.

F : It seems that it was a widespread practice for older, established members of the community, and especially the ones we would call "professors," to take a close interest in their young male disciples. The relationship between them would become extremely close and intense.

M : I would say so, if this included having sex with them!

F : Apparently that was usually the case. But I'm not so sure that we're very different.

M : What? How can you say that?

F : I mean, a lot of men in our society, and especially professors, play the same role to their own proteges. The only difference that I can see is that nowadays these are usually heterosexual relationships, not homosexual ones.

Questions

1. *Who was Plato? What did he write?*
2. *What does "platonic" mean when used to describe personal relationships?*
3. *Why do you suppose translators have distorted the original meaning?*

- **deliberate :** done or said on purpose; intentional
- **soften :** make or become soft or softer
- **palatable :** acceptable to the taste; agreeable
- **dumbfound :** make (sb) speechless with astonishment; amaze
- **disciple :** (sb) who accepts and helps to spread the teachings of a leader; follower
- **protege :** (sb) with the support, protection, or care of (sb) of importance
- **heterosexual :** having sexual feelings for members of the opposite sex
- **distort :** give a false report of (sth); misrepresent

Issue 20 Marrying Young

M : Remember when you were a teenager in love?

F : Do I! As though it were yesterday!

M : Everything was so intense then!

F : I'll say! I thought love was the greatest thing since ice cream.

M : Isn't it?

F : Mmmm. It's even better than ice cream. But I didn't know what real love was.

M : Yes. I had a real naive idea. I thought if a girl was cute and smiled at me, it must be love!

F : I was so shy that I didn't know if guys smiled at me or not.

M : I'll bet all the little boys were in love with you.

F : Hey! They weren't so little! We're talking about teenage romance, not kindergarten.

M : You're right. But I'm sure it didn't matter—kindergarten, high school, college—I know you were always a cutie.

F : Why, thank you! Don't flatter me so much.

M : No, I mean it.

F : I used to think that love was a boy and a girl looking at each other and blushing.

M : What? No kissing?

F : Not when I was a girl.

M : No holding hands?

F : Well. Maybe holding hands. A little.

M : Falling in love was so easy then.

F : It sure was. One time after another. I'd be sure that I was madly in love with someone, and then there'd be someone else that I loved even more!

M : So? What happened to these sweet dreams?

F : I guess we grew up and found out what real love really is.

- **intense** : deeply felt
- **I'll say** : Yes
- **cutie** : (sb) who is attractive and nice
- **mean (sth)** : be sincere about (sth)
- **blush** : become suddenly red in the face from modesty, embarrassment, or shame

M : And what is it, really?

F : You should know! You're married!

M : Do you think love is just working all day, paying the bills, hardly seeing each other and then getting into a fight when you do?

F : Heavens![↓] No! Love is learning to share your life with someone, raising a family, growing old together. Love is going through life and not being able to imagine not doing it with the one you love.

M : I guess your experience with love is a lot happier than mine.

F : I'm sorry to hear that.

M : The old, teenage version was better, I think.

F : I don't think so. It was just a nice fantasy that didn't have anything to do with the world we live in.

M : But it sure was a world I'd love to live in again, all the same.[↓]

Questions

1. How many definitions of "love" do you find?

2. How are their experiences with love different?

3. Which one is happier? How can you tell?

→ **Heavens! :** exclamatory statement of shock

→ **all the same :** despite what has been mentioned

Issue 21 Be

F : I went shopping today and spent three hours going from store to store until I found what I was looking for.

M : Oh! What did you get?

F : I didn't get anything.

M : What! Why not?

F : I thought it was just too expensive. If I wait a few months I can get the same thing and save some money.

M : A lot of money?

F : Well, "a lot" is relative, I guess. Probably 5 or 6%. But the point is that "a penny saved is a penny earned."

M : A penny! Is that all?

F : No, of course not. A few dollars, though.

M : But, in the meantime, you could still be using that article you took so long to find. What about all the time you wasted? "Time is money," you know.

F : That's true, but now I know where to look for it. I would have had to spend the same amount of time shopping for it in any event.

M : Don't be such a cheapskate!

F : I'm not cheap. I'm frugal. I don't like spending more money than I have to.

M : It sounds very noble, but the sums involved are trivial.

F : It all adds up. "A trip of many miles is achieved one step at a time."

M : "But don't make a mountain out of a molehill."

F : I don't like being called a "cheap Charlie."

M : "If the shoe fits, wear it."

F : When did this conversation devolve into the proverbial shouting match?

- molehill : small pile of earth made by a mole
- devolve : pass on

M : OK, you're right. We shouldn't fight about this. Especially since it's basically a question of semantics.

F : What do you mean?

M : Well, it's the difference between a denotation and a connotation.

F : I still don't understand.

M : A denotation is the dictionary definition; by this standard, "frugal," and "cheap," and "thrifty" are all synonyms. But a connotation is an emotional attitude conveyed by some word. So, while "cheap" and "frugal" may mean the same, one has a negative association and the other a positive one.

F : Oh! I see!

M : Do you know any other examples?

F : Well, let me think. I like you a lot, but sometimes I think you are very naive. When you are behaving in a sweetly innocent way, I guess I think of you as being childlike. But when you irritate me, like you just did, then I would say that you're too childish. Is that what you mean?

M : Ouch! I get your point. Why don't we talk about something else?

Questions

1. How are cheap and frugal different?

2. Why didn't the woman buy anything today?

3. What is the difference between one who is childlike and one who is childish?

- **semantics :** meaning or interpretation of a word, sign, etc.
- **denotation :** the specific meaning of a word or expression
- **connotation :** secondary meaning of a word or expression that comes to mind or is suggested in addition to its primary meaning
- **association :** idea suggested by or connected with (sth) else
- **naive :** showing a lack of experience or judgment

Issue 22 The New Work Regimen

M : Did you hear? The company is going to lay off 10% of its employees.

F : That's a lot of workers out of a job. I feel sorry for them. Who's going to feed their families?

M : It'll just be temporary, I'm sure. Most of them have valuable skills and a lot of experience, so they should be able to get new jobs pretty easily.

F : At the lower levels, perhaps. The ordinary workers are often the ones who can cope with the changed situation the easiest. But the mid-level managers will have it the hardest, I'm afraid.

M : Why do you think so?

F : Because they are not young enough to accept entry-level positions again, but they are not old enough to have gained enough savvy to take on a high-level executive job. Companies will hire younger new managers who are just getting started, or older highly-qualified upper bosses with much experience. They'll promote their own mid-level executives into higher positions and won't need new people to fill the middle.

M : In my mind, the situation looks like a bell-shaped curve. The youngest and least experienced people looking for jobs, and the extremely successful old ones, will have the highest rates of getting a job, and the ones in the middle will have the hardest time.

F : Exactly!

M : But don't you think it's different for non-executives? What about the ordinary workers?

F : If they have a skilled trade that is in demand, their age won't matter much at all. The well-experienced ones may make more money, but the new ones, with skills, won't have trouble finding jobs.

→ **lay off :** dismiss or suspend (sb) from a job
→ **savvy :** practical understanding; common sense

M : On the other hand, they're being punished unfairly by losing their jobs. It's not their fault that the company has been mismanaged. If the bosses had done their jobs correctly, nobody would be laid off.

F : The ones at the very top are the ones who made the bad decisions, but, because of their controlling positions they are not the ones who will have to leave. Unfortunately, their immediate subordinates↓ will pay the highest price.

Questions

1. Who is likely to be hurt the most? Why?

2. Who won't get harmed at all? Why?

3. Describe a bell-shaped curve.

→ **subordinate :** (sb) who has a lower position and less authority than someone else in an organization

Issue 23 Two Sides of the Same Coin

F : I just don't understand my husband!

M : Mmmmmmmmmmmmm.

F : I just can't get him to leave me alone.

M : Oh?

F : He doesn't seem concerned at all about my mood or schedule, as long as he is satisfied. I never have any time for myself.

M : What's wrong with that?

F : There's no romance left, our relationship is just very mechanical and one-sided.

M : My wife is just the opposite.

F : In what way?

M : She insists that I don't give her enough attention. I come home from work tired, she's on the phone. Hours later, she's still on the phone, and I go to bed by myself. Or, I get home and she's already in bed asleep. If I wake her up, she complains. But she insists that I don't pay enough attention to her needs. What about my needs—does she ever concern herself about those?

F : At least you're not a slob. I have to pick up after my husband every day. He never puts things away, just drops them where he is when he's finished and goes off somewhere else.

M : No, I'm more the compulsive orderly type, I guess. I just can't stand a mess! If there's something that needs to be cleaned up, I can't do a single thing until it's taken care of. It drives my wife crazy, but I can't help it. It's the way I am.

F : I think we married the wrong people! We should have tied the knot ourselves!

M : Well, it's too late now! I guess we just have to live with it.

Questions

1. How are their situations complementary?

2. How is the phone an inconvenience?

3. What is her solution to the problem?

- **slob :** dirty, lazy, or messy person
- **compulsive :** impossible to control
- **orderly :** correctly or neatly arranged or organized
- **We should have tied the knot ourselves :** We should have married each other
- **complementary :** supplying what is lacking or needed

Issue 24 Before You Kill Yourself

M : If you were able to choose your manner of death, what would it be?

F : What a morbid thought! Let's change the subject.

M : No, I'm serious. What is the best way of dying?

F : I guess some form of pills. Just go to sleep and never wake up. That would be painless and relatively peaceful.

M : Do you think so? Oftentimes, the system just rejects much of the poison. The would-be victim just vomits and defecates all over the bed, the body seizes up and twists in spasms. The result is hardly like "just going to sleep."

F : Ugh! That sounds terrible. Let me change my mind! What about you?

M : Well, if I were going to kill myself, maybe I'd put a bullet through my brain. It's quick and, well, dramatic.

F : But it's so gruesome! What about jumping from a bridge or high building?

M : That's certainly messy too, don't you think?. It's like they say, it's not the fall, it's the sudden stop that causes the damage! But I'm not necessarily thinking about suicide. If you were going to die naturally, what way would be the best?

- morbid : paying too much attention to death, decay, or other unhealthy matters
- defecate : get rid of solid waste from (one's) body
- seize up : suddenly stop moving or working properly
- spasm : sudden involuntary contraction of a muscle or group of muscles
- gruesome : causing horror and shock

F : Hmmmm. The worst way would be to burn up in a fire, that's for sure. But the best way? Maybe drowning?

M : As for me, I think the easiest way would be to freeze to death. The body slows down, the feeling fades away, and consciousness slowly disappears. You're dead even before you realize you're dying, painlessly. And you still look pretty normal when they recover your body in the spring thaw!

F : How did we get onto this subject anyway?

M : Oh, I don't know. One of my friends just died in a terrible automobile accident, and I can't stop thinking about how suddenly our lives may end.

F : Not all deaths are so terrible, you know. If I had my choice, I'd live to be a hundred and just fade away, surrounded by my friends and children. One moment, I'd be alive and alert, and the next, before anyone even knew it, I'd be gone!

M : Yep. That's the way to do it, all right! If only we all had that choice.

Questions

1. What are "good" ways to die? Why might they not be so good after all?

2. What horrible ways of dying are mentioned?

3. Why does he want to talk about dying? Does she want to?

thaw : period of warmer weather that melts ice and snow

Issue 25 The Real Person

F : Why do I have to be nice to my husband's family? We all know that I don't like them very much, and they sure don't care anything for me!

M : Well, you should at least try. It's only for a few hours every month. You might as well pretend to get along. It's better than fighting every time you meet. And think of your poor husband—he just gets caught right in the middle.

F : I don't regret at all that he loves his parents; I know that he loves me, too, so it's not a competition between us. But we've just never hit it off, and it's such a strain to put up with them. If he wanted to visit them by himself, I wouldn't mind at all. I could easily do something else while he was gone.

M : That's a terrible attitude!

F : You think so? Well, it's just the way I feel, that's all. I'm only being honest.

M : Honesty isn't always the best policy. If diplomats were completely honest with each other, there'd sure be a lot more wars and fewer international compromises.

F : But I'm not an ambassador. I'm just a person with a low tolerance for conformity just for the sake of conformity. We're all different people, and we shouldn't be ashamed of our true selves.

M : What if I told you that you were just a selfish, self-centered woman who cared more about her feelings than she did about her husband's needs? How would that make you feel?

F : Well, at least I'd know what you really thought about me. That's better than having the mistaken idea that you were my friend. Or, maybe, I'd realize that you were my true friend who wasn't afraid to tell me the truth. But, either way, a little true knowledge is better than any

- get caught in : be in a situation that is difficult
- hit it off : become friendly or close
- compromise : settlement of an argument in which each side gives up (sth)
- conformity : agreement; harmony

false belief.

M : Not many people can lead that kind of life. Most want to be comforted and reassured by their friends and colleagues. The world is cruel and heartless enough as it is.

F : I suppose you're right about that. But I'd rather deal with reality than fantasy. It's the way I was brought up.

M : To each his own, I guess. But I'm not that way myself. I'd rather avoid harsh reality if I could. I rather enjoy being coddled sometimes, even if it doesn't last.

F : That's not the way you seem to me, at all. What about what you said to me?

M : What did I say?

F : You said I was self-centered and indifferent to my husband's feelings!

M : No, I didn't. It was just a hypothetical question: "what if?" If you thought I meant that, I apologize.

F : OK, fine. But did you really mean it or not?

Questions

1. *Why would she rather keep away from her in-laws?*
2. *Why does society encourage dishonesty?*
3. *Why is (or is not) reality better than fantasy, according to each speaker?*

- **to each his own :** according to (one's) own custom, belief or idea
- **coddle :** treat tenderly or carefully; pamper
- **hypothetical :** theoretical; treating (sth) as if certain circumstances were real

APPENDIX

Openers for Your Discussion!

다음은 1:1 대화나 집단토론에서 자주 쓰이는 표현 (특히 처음 시작할 때의 표현을 중심으로)을 정리해 놓은 것입니다.

1) 모르는 사람에게 무엇인가를 묻기 위해접근해서 이야기를 걸때	Pardon me Sorry May I interrupt for a moment?	Excuse me Pardon me for interrupting, but
2) 집단 토론 중에 갑자기 지적할 문제가 생겨 말을 끊고 나올때	Sorry, but May I add something? May I ask a question? I'd like to comment on that I have a point here	I might add here May I say something here? Excuse me for interrupting, but I'd like to say something
3) 원래의 주제로 다시 돌아갈때	Anyway To return to To get back to Going back to What were we talking about?	In anycase Returning to Let's get back to Where was I?
4) 누군가에게 무엇을 물어볼때	I'd like to know Could you tell me Do you know	I'm interested in Could I ask Do you happen to know
5) 주저하거나 망설임을 나타낼때	Well Now You know	Look You see Listen
6) 일의 순서를 나열할때	First First of all	To begin with
	Secondly Then So Before you finish	Next After that So then
	At the end As the last thing	Finally

7) 중요한 점을 부각시킬때	First of all The most important thing is	The main thing is Primarily
8) 중요한 문제점을 지적할때	The trouble is Don't forget that The awful thing is	The problem is The real problem is
9) 놀랄만한 사실을 이야기 할때	Do you realize that Believe it or not It may sound strange (or funny), but Strangely enough	Surprisingly You may not believe this, but
10) 새로운 사실을 이야기 할때	Guess what! Do you know what?	I've got news for you! You won't believe this, but
11) 일반적인 사실을 이야기 할때	Generally As a rule usually On the average	By and large Normally Typically
12) 상대방에게 즐겁지 않은 사실을 이야기 하고자 할때	Actually To tell the truth To be blunt	But frankly To be honest
13) 현실적인 이야기를 하고자 할때	To be honest with you Now be realistic	Let's face it
14) 이야기의 주제를 바꿀때	Speaking of By the way I just thought of something	That reminds me Before I forget
15) 자기의견을 이야기 할때	I think In my opinion I personally think I suspect I'm almost positive	I imagine In my estimation To my mind I'm pretty sure I have reason to believe
16) 자기확신을 이야기 할때	I strongly believe I'm convinced Without a doubt	I'm positive Undoubtedly

17) 개인적인 상황을 이야기 할때	In my case Personally, I'm more interested in	What I'm concerned with is For my own part
18) 소문 따위의 비밀스런 이야기를 하고자 할때	I've heard Just between you and me I hear they say	They say Rumor has it
19) 어떤 제안을 하고자 할때	Why don't you If I were you, I would Perhaps you could Try May I make a suggestion	I suggest you Why not How about I have an idea
20) 어떤 계획에 대하여 이야기 하고자 할때	I'm planning to Our plan is to What we have in mind is What we plan to do is	What I'm planning to do is We are thinking of Our scheme is
21) 어떤 특정한 포인트에 대해 설명하고자 할대	Regarding As far as (something) is concerned Where (something) is concerned When it comes to (something) In that respect On that point	Concerning As far as that goes In that instance
22) 특정한 상황에 대해 의견을 말할때	In a case like this In a situation like this In this type of situation	In this case In such a situation In this instance
23) 어떤 특정한 포인트를 강조할때	That's just the point But the point is This raises a problem But the problem with that is	But the question is But the real question is This raises a question
24) 특정한 포인트를 추가할때	Also In addition In other respect Perhaps I should mention Not to mention the fact that Not only that, but	And another thing What's more I might add I almost forgot Plus the fact that

25) 이유를 설명할때	The reason why	The main reason why
	Owing to	Due to
	Because	Because of
	Since	
26) 제시된 이유에 대한 부연설명을 할때	For this reason	On account of this
	Owing to this	Because of this
	This is why	This is the reason why
	That's why	That's the reason why
	Therefore	So
	As a result	Consequently
	Thus	
27) 즉각적인 대답 보다는 약간 망설임을 나타낼때	Well, uhm	Well, let's see
	Let's put it this way	I'll have to think about that
28) 자기 자신의 의견 (또는 의미)을 분명히 할때	What I mean is	What I meant was
	What I'm saying is	What I'm trying to say is
	Don't get me wrong	
	Don't misunderstand me (on this point)	
	Let me put it another way	That's not what I said
	What I really said	
	You must have misunderstood me	
	Let's get this straight, I said	
29) 무엇인가를 거절할때	I don't care for	I can't stand
	I'm not going to	This isn't my idea of
	I don't like	I can't take
	What I can't stand is	
	I'm not really interested in	I'm not worried about
	I don't need	I have no use for
	I don't have the time to	I'm not concerned with
	I'm perfectly satisfied with	
	I'd prefer	I'd rather
30) 질문하고 무엇인가를 제안할때	I wonder why	Do you really think (or believe)
	Are you serious when you say	Isn't it true that
	Why do you	Do you mean to say

	Don't you think (or say, or agree) Wouldn't it be a good idea I wonder if	Wouldn't it be better Why don't you
31) 설명을 요구할때	Can you explain why I don't understand why Why is it that What do you mean by What do you have in mind (with)	I wonder why I keep wondering why Why do you think
32) 어떤 계획에 대해 유보적인 입장을 취할때	I doubt I don't know if Yes, but Sure, but I'd love to, but That may be so, but I don't see advantage in What I'm concerned about is What bothers me is One drawback is	I'm afraid But the problem is Possibly, but That's a good idea, but That would be great, except Yes, but the question is What I'm worried about is What I'm afraid of is What I don't like is
33) 어떤점을 고려하라고 할때	Considering Taking into account If you remember Allowing for the fact All things considered	Seeing Remembering Keeping in mind When you consider
34) 다른 대안이 없어 굴복할때	If there's no other way If that's so Well, under those circumstances	If there's no alternative
35) 빈도 (Frequency)를 나타낼때	Generally As a rule Ordinarily Usually Again and again Once in a while From time to time	In general Mostly As a general rule Most of the time Time and again Every so often Every now and then

36) 예외를 지적할때

There are exceptions, of course
One should mention, of course
An exception to that is, of course
This does not include
Except that
But what about
With the exception of (that)
One exception is
But think of

37) 예를 들고자 할때

For example
Take for example
For one thing
To illustrate my point
As an illustration
For instance
A classic example of this is
To give you an idea
Just as an example

38) 요약 및 결론을 이야기 할때

To make a long story short
So you see
So
In the end
To sum up
Summing up
To put it in a nutshell
In brief
So in short
So finally
All in all
To conclude
To summarize
To put it into a few words
In a nutshell

39) 동의를 나타낼때

That's right
Okay
Yes
I agree (with you)
That's true
I guess so
Right
Correct
Exactly
You're right
I know

That's just what I was thinking.
That's exactly what I was thinking.
I couldn't agree with you more.
That's exactly what I think.
My feelings exactly.
You can say that again.
I see your point.
I feel the same way.
I'll say
That's a good point.

40) 반대를 나타낼때

That's ridiculous
Aw, come on!
What!
Are you kidding?
What do you mean?

	I don't believe it	No, definitely not
	Are you pulling my leg?	That doesn't fit.
	I disagree	I don't agree
	I don't think so	I don't think that's fair
	I'm not sure	I hate to disagree with you, but
41) 불행한 사건에 대해 반응할때	Oh no	That's too bad
	What a pity	What a shame
	What a nuisance	Poor you
	How awful	How terrible
	That must have been awful	I'm sorry to hear that
	Oh, my God	
42) 예상했던(당연한) 불행한 결과에 대한 반응	It's your own fault	Someday you'll learn
	That'll teach you	Serves you right
	What else did you expect?	
43) 상대방의 말에 흥미를 보일때	Right	Okay
	Yeah	Yes?
	And?	Well?
	Really?	And then?
	And so?	Mh-hmm
	Uh-huh	
44) 반복을 요청할때	Pardon me?	I beg your pardon?
	Could you say that again?	
	Would you repeat that, please?	
	Sorry?	
	Would you mind repeating that?	You lost me there
	I didn't catch that last part.	What's that again?
	Sorry, I don't follow you.	I'm lost.
	I didn't get that.	
45) 전화상에서 상대방에게 반복을 요구할때	Sorry, what did you say?	Pardon?
	I'm sorry I didn't understand that.	
	Do you mind repeating that?	
	Can you repeat that for me, please?	
	Sorry?	

46) 상대방의 이해정도를 확인할 때	Are you following me? Is that clear? Are you coming along fine? Got it?	Are you with me? Okay so far? Do you understand so far? Right?
47) 상대방의 칭찬에 대한 답을 할때	Oh, thank you Kind of you to say that Do you really think so? I'm flattered. That's nice to hear	Oh, thanks That's very kind of you Thanks, I needed that. Oh, I'm glad you think so.
48) 더이상 이야기할 시간이 없을때	Sorry, I've got to go I must be going I hope you don't mind, but	I have to run Would you excuse me, please?
49) 전화한 사람이 끊을려고 할때	I'd better let you go I know you are busy, so I'll let you go It's been good talking to you	Thanks for your time
50) 전화 받은 사람이 끊을려고 할때	Well, thanks for calling I'm afraid I don't have time to talk I appreciate your calling	

LIS KOREA에서 나온
DISCUSSION TEXTBOOK

LIS KOREA는 토론학습 교재전문 출판사입니다.

설명간결한 형식의 새로운 토론교재

Express Yourself Directly (1), (2)

- Pictures Talk 섹션에서는 큰 주제에 대한 warm-up 주제들을 선정하여 그림과 함께 제시하여 본주제에 쉽게 접근할 수 있도록 했습니다.
- Express Yourself Directly 섹션에서는 Pictures Talk 섹션에서 다루지 않은 좀더 깊은 주제를 선정하여 심도있는 토론이 되도록 했습니다.
- Let's Talk Funny 섹션에서는 본 주제와 관련 있는 재미있는 이야기를 실어 가벼운 토론과 함께 긴장을 풀도록 했습니다.
- What Does It Mean? 에서는 본 주제와 관련된 Food For Thought 를 제공하여 학습자들이 자유롭게 토론 할수 있도록 했으면 다양한 의견이 나올 수 있는 문구 들을 제시하였습니다.
- 마지막으로 Synopsis 에서는 (전체 400의 그림으로 구성) 각 그림에 대한 설명을 영어로 명쾌하게 제시하여 학습자로 하여금 주제에 대한 최종 복습을 할 수 있도록 했습니다.를 제공합니다.

청소년의 세계와 그들의 생각 관심사들을 토론으로

Chat Room for Teens (1)(2)(3)

- New Children's Talk를 배운 학생들이 Teen Talk를 쉽게 익힐 수 있는 선행학습교재로 사용할 수 있도록 구성
- 학습의 재미와 능률을 높이기 위해 다향한 그림들과 그것들을 바탕으로한 토론들 그리고 실제 많은 상황에서 발생하는 대화들과 수많은 지문들을 바탕으로 토론의 다양성을 확보

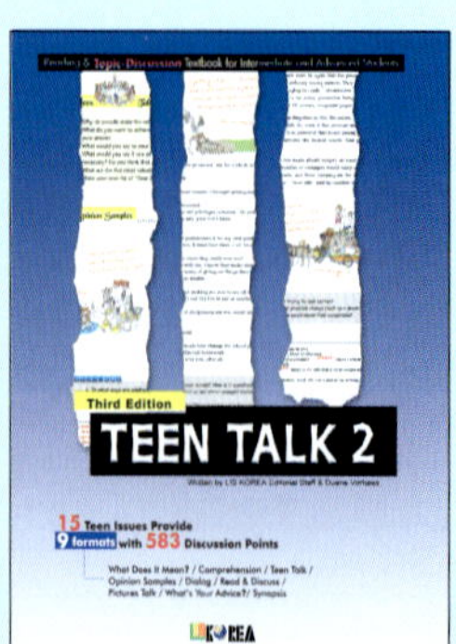

청소년을 위한 토론교재

New Teen Talk (1), (2)

- 청소년 토론교재의 최고 높은 단계의 교재로서 각권 15개의 이슈속에 500개 이상의 토론주제를 제시합니다.
- 각 권에 포함된 9개의 포멧은 (What Does It Mean?/ Comprehension/ Teen Talk / Opinion Samples/ Dialog/ Read& Discuss/ Pictures Talk / What's Your Advice? /Synopsis/) 각각의 특징에 맞는 다양하고 흥미로운 토론 주제를 제공합니다.

Inside Let's Talk (2)

CONTENTS

Let's Talk (1)

초판 8쇄 인쇄 : 2016년 1월 5일 인쇄
초판 8쇄 발행 : 2016년 1월 10일 발행
지 은 이 : 리스코리아 편집부 & Duane Vorhees
그 림 : 일러스트레이터 박희정
펴 낸 곳 : (도서출판) 리스코리아
펴 낸 이 : 조은예
등 록 : 남양주 제 399-2011-000003호
전 화 : (0502) 423-7947
편 집 디 자 인 : 예림칼라
인 쇄 : (주)미광원색사
www.liskorea.co.kr